# Clueless in the Kitchen

## Cooking for Beginners

## Evelyn Raab

FIREFLY BOOKS

# A FIREFLY BOOK

Published by Firefly Books Ltd. 2017
Copyright © 2017 Firefly Books Ltd.
Text copyright © 2017 by Evelyn Raab
Photographs © 2017 by Mike McColl

First printing

**Publisher Cataloging-in-Publication Data (U.S.)**
Names: Raab, Evelyn, author.
Title: Clueless In the Kitchen : Cooking for Beginners / Evelyn Raab.
Description: Richmond Hill, Ontario, Canada : Firefly Books, 2017.| Includes index. | Summary: This book contains basic cooking techniques and simple recipes using few processed foods.
Identifiers: ISBN 978-1-77085-933-3 (paperback)
Subjects: LCSH: Cooking.
Classification: LCC TX652.R333 |DDC 641.512 – dc23

**Library and Archives Canada Cataloguing in Publication**
A CIP record for this title is available from Library and Archives Canada

Published in the United States by
Firefly Books (U.S.) Inc.
P.O. Box 1338, Ellicott Station
Buffalo, New York  14205

Published in Canada by
Firefly Books Ltd.
50 Staples Avenue, Unit 1
Richmond Hill, Ontario  L4B 0A7

Cover and interior design: Marijke Friesen
Food styling: Maria Bachmaier

Printed in China

# Canada

We acknowledge the financial support of the Government of Canada.

# Table of Contents

# Starting from Scratch

How you ended up with this book is not important. Maybe your parents gave it to you. Maybe you bought it for yourself. Maybe you found it in a ditch. It doesn't matter. The thing is, you have it. And now you have to use it. But how?

So, this is a cookbook. You've probably already noticed that. And it's full of recipes — which is pretty much what you'd expect. These recipes are simple without being stupid. They contain no scary terminology, no really weird ingredients, no complicated procedures. They also contain (almost) no processed foods — no cake mixes, no instant soup, no fake whipped topping. You don't need them. Ever. Cooking from scratch is easy and cheap and *always* tastes better. That's a fact.

This book is full of other stuff you need to know too. Kitchen stuff. Basic information that no one ever bothered to tell you. Or maybe you weren't listening. And now you're sorry, because *now* you want to know. *Now* the kitchen needs sanitizing, or *now* you need to cut up a chicken or have to (*yikes!*) convert measurements. And you certainly don't want to go crawling back home, do you? You'll also find info on how to shop, where to find specialty items and how to plan a meal.

So how do you get started? Well, just start. Find something you want to cook and cook it. Go ahead — be brave. After all, cooking isn't brain surgery. It just looks like it.

# How to Cook Absolutely Anything

**Read the recipe.** Twice. The first time — to decide if the dish actually sounds like something you want to cook. Or eat. Does the recipe include an ingredient you hate? Does it require a piece of equipment you don't have? Do you have enough time to cook it? The second time — read the recipe more c-a-r-e-f-u-l-l-y. Do you have all the ingredients? Are you sure? Didn't you use up all the chocolate chips last week? Go check. Now.

**Assemble everything you need before you start.** Everything. The bowls, the pots, the measuring cups and all the ingredients. Take nothing for granted. You don't want to discover at a critical moment that the baking dish you need is in the freezer, half filled with last week's leftover lasagna.

**Follow the recipe exactly.** This is no time to be rebellious. At least, not the first time. Make it once *exactly* the way the recipe tells you to. Just once. The next time, go ahead and be reckless. Leave out the tomatoes! Double the walnuts! Heck — add some peanut butter! It's your recipe now, baby.

**Get over disasters.** Everyone has them. Don't let yourself wallow in yours. Pick yourself up, scrape the burned crud off the bottom of the oven, mop up the mess on the floor, feed the disintegrated glop to the dog. And get on with life. It happens.

**Know what you like.** You can't cook if you don't know what you like to eat. And eating, after all, is the goal. Know what you enjoy eating, cook what you want to eat and you'll probably have fun cooking.

**And finally — there are no rules.** No one owns a recipe and there is no right or wrong way for something to taste. If you like it, then it's good. If you don't like it, then it's not good. That's all there is to it. Trust yourself.

# The Kitchen
## A Guide to Alien Territory

## Totally Essential Kitchen Stuff You Really Need

- large frying pan
  (10 inches/25 cm diameter) or larger
- large pot (6 quarts/liters) or larger
  *with* a lid (a heavy Dutch oven is
  very useful)
- microwave-safe casserole
  (2 to 3 quarts/liters) with a lid
- large sharp knife
- wooden spoon for cooking
- muffin pan (12-cup)
- set of measuring spoons
- pot holders or oven mitts

- small frying pan
  (6 inches/15 cm diameter) or thereabouts
- small saucepan (2 1/2 quarts/liters)
- strainer or colander
- at least 2 mixing bowls — one large
  and one small (and more is better)
- small sharp paring knife
- wooden cutting board
- cookie sheet (2, if possible)
- measuring cup
- grater
- can opener

## Very Nice to Have, but Not Essential

- a really big stock pot
  for making a huge vat
  of soup or spaghetti
  sauce
- vegetable peeler
- electric mixer
- toaster
- metal spatula (turner)

- kitchen scissors
- roasting pan
- loaf pan
- soup ladle
- wire whisk
- microwave oven
- wok
- garlic press

- heavy cast iron frying pan
- collapsible vegetable steamer
- pie pan
- metal tongs
- blender
- food processor
- rubber or silicone scraper
- potato masher

**A** cookie sheets
**B** set of measuring spoons
**C** potato masher
**D** wooden spoon for cooking
**E** wire whisk

**F** large pot
**G** small saucepan
**H** microwave-safe casserole with a lid
**I** soup ladle
**J** large and small frying pan

**K** collapsible vegetable steamer
**L** strainer or colander
**M** mixing bowls
**N** pot holders or oven mitts
**O** measuring cup
**P** grater
**Q** metal spatula (turner)
**R** rubber or silicone scraper
**S** loaf pan
**T** muffin pan (12-cup)
**U** vegetable peeler
**V** small sharp paring knife
**W** large sharp knife
**X** metal tongs
**Y** can opener
**Z** wooden cutting board

## Storing Food — What Should Go Where

You bought it — now where do you keep it? Rule of thumb: When in doubt, keep it in the fridge. Except, of course, if it's frozen.

### In the cupboard or pantry

- flour and sugar
- unopened jars of jam, mayonnaise, pickles, salad dressing, condiments
- vegetable oils, olive oil
- pasta, rice, grains, beans
- chocolate
- onions and garlic
- soup mixes
- nuts (or refrigerate for longer storage)
- canned foods
- vinegar
- spices and dried herbs
- potatoes
- cookies, cake

### In the fridge

- eggs
- cooked leftovers
- most dairy products (yogurt, sour cream, etc.)
- open jars of jam, mayonnaise, ketchup, pickles, salad dressing, condiments
- cheese
- meat, fish, poultry
- bread (for longer storage)
- most fresh vegetables and fruit

### In the freezer

- baked things — bread, cakes, cookies (anything you won't be using soon)
- ice cream
- frozen foods, obviously

## Basic Kitchen Sanitation — A Matter of Life and Death

You *definitely* don't want food poisoning. Besides being totally disgusting, it could actually kill you. Which is obviously not a good thing. So how do you avoid this experience? The following food-handling safety tips will help.

**Don't thaw frozen foods on the kitchen counter.** Bacteria grow quickly at room temperature, rapidly turning your ground beef into a toxic time bomb. Thaw frozen meat overnight in the refrigerator or defrost in the microwave just before cooking.

**When in doubt, throw it out!** If meat or other food looks or smells weird, cooking *will not* make it safe to eat. Just get rid of it and order a pizza instead.

**Keep your work areas clean.** This isn't just a clean-freak thing — it's an actual safety thing. Wash your hands, cutting board and utensils in hot, soapy water before and after messing around with food. Cross-contamination is a real danger. It happens when bacteria-laden juices from raw meat or poultry contact a surface (like your cutting board, knife or hands) that then contaminates another food (such as bread or lettuce). Keep cooked and raw foods entirely separate and wash or sanitize all cooking utensils and surfaces after using. It's better to be crazy clean than sick.

**Forget the rare hamburger.** Just forget about it. Ground meats — beef, chicken, pork, turkey — are especially dangerous, because when meat is ground, the outer surface (which may be teeming with bacteria) is mixed throughout the meat. Cook any type of ground meat until you can no longer see any pink, and don't even think about eating any of that stuff raw.

**Don't let cooked foods hang around at room temperature.** Keep cold foods cold and hot foods hot. That leftover lasagna? Stick it right into the fridge — don't leave it loitering on the counter.

**Watch that potato salad!** Keep all salads that are made with eggs or mayonnaise refrigerated until serving time. Going on a picnic? Use a vinaigrette dressing instead of mayo — you'll find one in this book. How embarrassing if you poisoned Aunt Mildred.

# Shopping

You're hungry. You're in the mood to cook something. You're not in the mood to go shopping. If you keep a few basic groceries on hand, you'll always be able to whip something up.

## Kitchen staples

- flour
- salt and pepper
- oatmeal
- bouillon cubes or powder
- baking powder
- milk
- potatoes
- peanut butter
- apples

- sugar
- rice
- chocolate chips
- pasta
- canned tomatoes
- baking soda
- onions
- garlic
- jam
- butter or margarine

- coffee and tea
- vegetable oils /olive oil
- canned beans
- spaghetti sauce
- canned tuna and salmon
- eggs
- carrots
- bread
- cheese
- cinnamon

## Supermarket strategies

Supermarkets are in the business of selling as much stuff as they possibly can. And they do it very well. When you go shopping, be aware of the booby traps that await an unsuspecting consumer — and avoid them.

**Big rule: Never shop hungry.** Eat something *(anything)* before you step a single toe inside the supermarket, or else you'll find yourself buying things you would normally be able to resist. If you don't think this is true, just try to walk down the bakery aisle when you haven't eaten lunch.

**Buy store-label brands.** These are usually cheaper than name-brand products and often just as good. In fact, you might even like the store-brand potato chips better than your usual kind.

**Buy big only when it makes sense.** If you can't use up that humongous jar of jam before it goes bad, then it doesn't make sense to buy it. On the other hand, if a five-pound bag of carrots costs just a few cents more than a two-pound bag, go for it — just don't forget to eat the carrots.

**Beware the ends of the aisles.** Don't assume that just because something is displayed at the end of an aisle it's on sale. Sometimes it's not. Very sneaky. Check the price.

**Buy only what you really need.** Make a list at home and take it with you to the store. If you just need milk and a loaf of bread, go straight for those items, pay for them and leave the store. Immediately. Do not walk past the cookies. Do not linger at the ice cream.

**Don't buy three peppers if you only want one.** If the store has wrapped fresh vegetables into packages of two or more, ask the produce person (nicely) to (please) remove one pepper and price it for you. Produce people *will* do that.

**Check the dates on perishable items.** Dairy products such as milk and yogurt, baked goods like bread and rolls, and many other perishable foods are marked with a Best Before date. This just means what it says — the item is best before a certain date. It does not mean that the item is automatically rotten the next day — but it might be. Always look for items with the latest Best Before date to get the freshest stock.

**Don't even glance at the junk around the checkout counter.** This is where they put all the stuff no one needs. They are counting on you to surrender to impulse and buy a chocolate bar or a magazine or a pack of gum. You are being manipulated! You must resist!

## Recipe abbreviation decoder

Recipes tend to use a lot of abbreviations. You'll need to know the difference between tsp. and tbsp. if you want those cookies to turn out perfectly. Here's some help.

| | |
|---|---|
| tsp. — teaspoon | tbsp. — tablespoon |
| lb. — pound | gal. — gallon |
| qt. — quart | pt. — pint |
| fl. oz. — fluid ounce | oz. — ounce |
| (volume measurement) | (weight measurement) |
| ml — milliliter | g — gram |
| kg — kilogram | cm — centimeter |
| l — liter | F — Fahrenheit |
| C — Celsius | |

# How to Buy Fruits and Vegetables

It's a jungle out there! Step into the produce section of any supermarket and you're instantly overwhelmed. There are oranges and apples and grapes and bananas. There are onions and eggplants and tomatoes and seven kinds of lettuce. There are fruits you've never seen before and stuff you don't know what to do with. So? What are you waiting for — an engraved invitation? Go buy something. Here are some words of wisdom to help you navigate this confusing area.

**Fresh fruits and vegetables should look and smell fresh.** They should be firm and shiny, with no rotten spots. This doesn't mean you can't use an apple with a bruise on it, or a slightly droopy string bean. But if you're paying top dollar for fresh produce, look it over carefully to make sure it really is worth buying. If it isn't, don't buy it.

**Whenever possible, buy what's in season.** It will likely be inexpensive and better quality than out-of-season produce. Eat apples in the fall, oranges in the winter, asparagus in the spring and peaches in the summer.

**Buy locally grown fruits and vegetables whenever possible.** Why would anyone buy imported tomatoes in August when the local ones are delicious and abundant? Ask questions and shop smart.

**Shop at farmers' markets whenever you can.** Getting involved with your cauliflower is easy when you've talked to the guy who grew it. And there's no better way to make sure the stuff is really fresh. Plus, it's a great way to learn about local food. You might even get some ideas for how to cook what you've bought.

**Don't buy more than you can possibly use.** Buying a huge basket of fresh peaches is pointless if you can't eat them all before they rot.

**Check out the clearance bin!** Sometimes you can find wonderful bargains. Lots of marked-down produce is perfect if you plan to eat it or cook with it right away. The bin is a haven for banana bread bakers and soup lovers.

**Buy Brussels sprouts even if you think you hate them.** Just once. Maybe you hate them because of how your grandma cooked them. Maybe you'll *love* them the way you cook them. You'll never know unless you try. This also goes for squash.

**Who cares what it is — just try it!** No vegetable will kill you, even if you eat one raw that should have been cooked, or cooked one better left raw. Even a potato eaten raw isn't toxic — although it may be unusual. So don't be afraid of buying something unfamiliar just because you don't know what to do with it. Think of it as an opportunity to do some potentially delicious research and experimentation.

# Eat right — stay healthy!

These basic guidelines can help make sure that you're eating a healthy, nutritious diet. There is enough flexibility built in to allow for the little idiosyncracies that make us all so wonderfully unique, and it can be adapted for either a meat-eating or vegetarian diet.

The following is an outline of the complete dietary requirements for a single day. You don't have to fit every single food group into every single meal. Instead, take your eating habits over the whole day into consideration, including snacks. If you're a grazer who eats small amounts all day long, just total everything you eat and make sure it adds up. You could, theoretically, have all your grain servings at breakfast, all your fruit for lunch and everything else for dinner. It would be weird, but you could do it. Or else you can have normal meals with a little of each type of food on your plate at the same time. Suit yourself.

The guide is designed for a healthy, average adult. And keep in mind that nutritional guidelines are constantly changing as we learn more about how our bodies develop. Keep up to date on the latest information, both in print and online, if you want to make sure you're eating right.

## VEGETABLES AND FRUITS

7 to 10 servings per day
Fresh, frozen or canned vegetables or fruit, or fruit or vegetable juice
**Serving size:** 1 medium whole fruit (apple, orange, banana); ½ cup (125 ml) chopped raw or cooked vegetables; ½ cup (125 ml) fruit or vegetable juice; 1 cup (250 ml) leafy salad; ¼ cup (60 ml) dried fruit

## GRAIN PRODUCTS

6 to 8 servings per day (make at least half of these whole grain)
Bread, cereal, rice and pasta
**Serving size:** 1 slice bread; ½ bagel, pita or tortilla; ½ cup (125 ml) cooked pasta, couscous or rice; 1 oz. (30 g) cold cereal; ¾ cup (175 ml) hot cereal

## MEAT AND ALTERNATIVES

2 to 3 servings per day
Fish, shellfish, poultry, lean meats, legumes (like beans and lentils), nuts, seeds, soy products (like tofu or tempeh), eggs
**Serving size:** ½ cup (125 ml) meat, poultry or fish; ¾ cup (175 ml) cooked beans, lentils, tofu or tempeh; 2 eggs; 2 tbsp. (30 ml) peanut butter or nut butters; ¼ cup (60 ml) shelled nuts and seeds

## MILK AND ALTERNATIVES

2 to 4 servings per day
Milk, yogurt, soft cheeses (like ricotta or cottage cheese), hard cheeses (like cheddar or Swiss)
**Serving size:** 1 cup (250 ml) milk or fortified soy beverage; ¾ cup (175 ml) yogurt or kefir; ½ cup (125 ml) cottage or ricotta cheese; 1½ oz. (45 g) hard cheese

## ALSO

2 to 3 tbsp. (30 to 45 ml) unsaturated vegetable oils or soft margarines that are low in saturated fats

# Cheese Shopping — An Adventure

There are (approximately) seventeen zillion types of cheese in the world. So why do you always buy that flat, plastic-wrapped kind? Why not take a chance and try a tiny wedge of something new? Hey, you might even fall in love!

The following extremely incomplete list will give you a start on your cheese adventures. After that, you're on your own.

### For slicing and in sandwiches

Monterey Jack, Havarti, Muenster, brick, cheddar, Colby, Edam, Emmentaler, Swiss, Jarlsberg, fontina, Gouda, provolone, Asiago

### For cooking, melting and casseroles

Monterey Jack, mozzarella, cheddar, Colby, Emmentaler, Swiss, Jarlsberg, fontina, Parmesan, Romano, Gruyère

### On crackers for a snack or appetizer

Brie, Camembert, Havarti, Muenster, Saint Paulin, cheddar, Colby, Stilton blue, Edam, Emmentaler, Swiss, Jarlsberg, Gouda, goat cheese

### In salads

Parmesan, feta, cheddar, goat cheese, Danish blue, Roquefort, bocconcini

# The Freezer Zone

What lurks behind the glass doors of your supermarket's freezer section? Well, almost everything, really.

The frozen food section of a supermarket is a minefield. If you're not careful, you can end up with lots of overpriced, overprocessed junk. But if you are careful, you can find plenty of stuff that's inexpensive, nutritious and convenient. Tread carefully and you'll be fine.

**Buy frozen foods that are as close to their original state as possible.** This means that frozen fish fillets can be a good choice, but frozen breaded fish fillets with marinara sauce and pizza cheese may not be. Plain frozen peas are excellent, but boil-in-the-bag peas with French onion gravy are not. The less processing a frozen food has endured, the less junk will have been added to it and the cheaper (and better) it will be.

**Stay away — far away — from frozen dinners.** Sure, the trays are cute and in ten minutes you've got a total meal. With dessert, even. But it's not worth it. The food is almost always overprocessed, overcooked and overpriced. In a big hurry to eat? You're better off to scramble an egg, cut up a tomato and toast a bagel. Need dessert? Have an apple.

**What about frozen pizza?** Well, it's cheaper than ordering in and sometimes it's decent enough. So, okay, keep one in the freezer for an emergency. As a main dish, when it's been one of those days, a pizza beats a bag of potato chips — just don't make a regular habit of it. Other items that might be handy to keep in your freezer: prepared beef or chicken pot pie or a frozen veggie lasagna.

## Junk food — or is it?

What is junk food, anyway? Is pizza bad? Or is it good? Are French fries junk? And what about gummy worms? How's a person to know?

Junk food is any food that doesn't contain enough nutrients to make it worth its weight in calories. Some junk food doesn't contain *any* nutrients. Any food high in sugar or fat, with very little redeeming protein, vitamins or fiber (gummy worms, sorry) is probably junk. On the other hand, pizza — which *can* be pretty salty and high in fat — is still okay (in moderation) because it also happens to be loaded with vegetables, cheese and other good stuff like that.

Occasionally a food gets a bad reputation just because it hangs around with the wrong crowd. Popcorn, for instance. Drench it in butter and salt and it's junky. Microwave popcorn is often overly salty and too high in fat. But get it on its own or with a sprinkle of cheese and a little salt, and it's a different snack altogether, high in fiber and low in calories. And it still tastes good. Actually, better.

Then there are the junk foods *pretending* to be good for you — like granola bars and chewy fruit snacks. Many commercial granola bars are too high in sugar and fat to be a *really* nutritious snack. And the ones covered with chocolate are, let's face it, chocolate bars. Fruit snacks are candy. Period. If you want a treat, have one of these. If you want fruit — have a real piece of fruit.

How should you make your choices?

Well, first read the ingredients. Is sugar heading the list? Junk. If you really want some junk, have it and get it over with. Then eat good stuff for the rest of the day. You don't have to give up eating chocolate bars and cheese puffs completely in order to have a healthy diet. Just don't let junk food *be* your diet. After all, you are what you eat. A scary thought, isn't it?

# Alternative Shopping

The supermarket isn't the only place to get food. It isn't even a particularly interesting place to get food. Branch out a little. Explore an Asian grocery. Investigate your local farmers' market. Be bold — buy something you don't recognize from a street vendor. Shop on the edge.

## International grocery stores

There are Asian grocery stores, Middle Eastern grocery stores and Indian grocery stores. There are shops that sell Latin American foods and shops that sell Italian foods. Every city has a few shops (sometimes entire neighborhoods) that carry products used in the cooking of a particular country or region. The shopkeepers are often delighted to share their culinary secrets — you may come away with a bagful of strange groceries and a few interesting recipes to go with them. Or go online to hunt down recipes for your favorite ethnic dishes and then go shopping for the ingredients. Either way you're guaranteed a delicious adventure.

## Farmers' markets

Farmers' markets can supply you with four kinds of beans, six kinds of potatoes, three kinds of cucumbers — did you even know they existed? Eggs that are white, brown or blue, locally produced honey and ultra hot pepper sauce. How can you resist buying a basket of peaches from the person who picked them? Talk to the pie lady or the organic chicken people or the goat cheese guys and you may just learn a little something. Get up early, hike out to your local farmers' market and check out what's growing these days.

## Your friend the bulk food store

So you buy a jar of oregano. The oregano weighs half an ounce. The jar (the jar!) weighs over four ounces. Does this make sense? What are you buying, anyhow — the jar or what's inside it? The dried herbs and spices sold in supermarkets are notoriously overpackaged. Buy herbs and spices from a bulk food store and keep them in airtight recycled jars, and you'll save money while you cut down on garbage.

Buy exactly the amount you need. Don't buy a one-pound bag of walnuts when you really only need a few. On the other hand, if you really go through the chocolate chips (and who doesn't?), keep a big jar filled with them to avoid those emergency trips to the corner convenience store.

Buying in bulk is cheaper. You'll save about 30 percent over the supermarket price on most items when you shop at a bulk food store. Pretty amazing when you think about it.

Bring your own bags when you go shopping, and whenever possible refill your own containers. Hooray for less waste!

# Those Scary Herbs and Spices

They *are* scary. There are too many of them, and you never have the one you need. The mere mention of *coriander* causes your hands to shake (see, it's happening already). Never mind *cardamom*. Help!

## Bare bones spice collection

**What can't you do without?**
salt and pepper

**What else?**
basil
oregano
cinnamon
paprika
fresh garlic
fresh parsley

**Want to add just a few more?**
cayenne pepper
curry powder
ginger
cumin
thyme
vanilla
Mexican chili powder

Okay, calm down. Deep-dark-secret: There isn't a single recipe that won't work anyway if you leave out every single herb and spice. Not that you *should* leave them all out, but you *can*. The food won't taste the same, but it will still be edible. You can also put in more or less of an herb than the recipe calls for and, even more shocking, you can substitute an entirely different herb or spice altogether if you want to.

So do something wild. Use cumin instead of caraway! Substitute oregano for basil! Leave out the cinnamon! Double the curry powder!

Look at you go! And you didn't think you were the reckless type.

# Appetizers, Snacks, Munchies and Starters

Whatever you want to call them, these bits and bites can be served *before* a meal, they can fill that pesky void *between* meals or sometimes they can actually *be* the whole meal all by themselves.

# Quesadillas

*A serious snack that comes dangerously close to being a meal.*

2 large (9-inch/25 cm) flour tortillas
¼ cup (60 ml) prepared salsa — mild, medium or hot
½ cup (125 ml) shredded Monterey Jack or cheddar cheese
Other toppings — jalapeños? Olives? Chocolate chips? (just kidding)

Place one tortilla on a flat surface and spread evenly with the salsa, leaving about 1/2 inch (1 cm) bare around the edges. Sprinkle with shredded cheese and whatever other toppings, if any, you might want to add. Slap the second tortilla on top and press the two together.

Lay the tortilla "sandwich" in a large, dry frying pan — no butter or oil or anything. Place over medium heat and cook, spinning it occasionally to keep it from sticking, until the cheese begins to melt (lift an edge and peek inside). Using a spatula, flip the quesadilla and cook the other side for 1 or 2 minutes, until the tortilla begins to brown and the cheese inside is completely melted. Slide onto a plate and cut into wedges like a pizza.

Makes 1 quesadilla. Repeat as needed.

## Logical quesadilla deviations
- Use spaghetti sauce instead of salsa, mozzarella cheese instead of Monterey Jack and sprinkle with some chopped pepperoni. Voilà! A pizzadilla.
- Add some shredded cooked chicken, pork or beef for something a little more substantial.
- Skip the salsa altogether and sprinkle the flour tortilla with crumbled feta cheese and raw baby spinach leaves. Cook just long enough to melt the cheese and wilt the spinach.
- Canned black beans? Leftover chili? Sloppy Joe meat? It's all good.

# Tomato and Basil Bruschetta   serves 4–5

*Make this in the summer when tomatoes have real flavor and fresh basil is easy to find.*

3 perfectly ripe medium tomatoes
2 cloves garlic, minced or pressed
2 tbsp. (30 ml) chopped fresh basil leaves
1 tsp. (5 ml) salt
¼ tsp. (1 ml) black pepper
1 long French baguette or crusty Italian bread
¼ cup (60 ml) olive oil

Preheat the broiler element of your oven. Place the top oven rack in the highest possible position.

Chop the tomatoes as finely as you can and put them in a mixing bowl. Add the garlic, basil, salt and pepper. Mix well.

With a sharp bread knife, cut the bread crosswise in half, then cut each half in half lengthwise. This will give you 4 long slabs of bread. Lay them, cut-side up, on a large cookie sheet or baking pan. Using a pastry brush (or clean paint-brush), brush the cut side of each slab of bread with some of the olive oil. Place on the top oven rack under the preheated broiler and toast the top of the bread for 3 to 5 minutes, just until golden brown. Don't leave the room. Don't check your email. Don't do anything. One minute too long under the broiler and the bread is charcoal. Remove from the oven immediately.

Spoon the tomato mixture over the toasted bread, cut into 3-inch (7 cm) chunks and serve to your adoring fans.

This really makes 4 or 5 servings as an appetizer, but you might just find yourself eating the whole business by yourself for dinner. Not a bad thing, really.

## Bruschetta variations

- Sprinkle some grated Parmesan cheese over the tomato mixture.
- Top the toasted bread with thinly sliced fresh mozzarella cheese (bocconcini) before adding the tomatoes.
- Add a chopped fresh hot pepper to the tomato mixture.
- Lay a thin slice of prosciutto on the toasted bread before topping with the tomato mixture.

# High-Voltage Garlic Bread serves 4–6

*This is serious garlic bread and should be treated with respect. Serve it with a big tossed salad, some homemade lasagna or a bowl of delicious minestrone soup.*

1 long French baguette or crusty Italian bread
4 to 6 cloves garlic, minced or pressed
2 tbsp. (30 ml) olive oil
2 tbsp. (30 ml) chopped fresh parsley
2 tbsp. (30 ml) grated Parmesan cheese
½ tsp. (2 ml) paprika (optional, but pretty)

Preheat oven to 400°F (200°C).

In a small bowl, combine the garlic and oil, mashing them together well. In another bowl, mix the chopped parsley, Parmesan cheese and paprika, if you're using it.

With a sharp bread knife, cut the bread into two equal halves, then cut each half in half horizontally as evenly as you can (don't obsess — it's only bread). This will give you 4 long slabs of bread. Brush the garlic-oil mixture onto the cut surfaces of the bread, using it all up. Sprinkle with the parsley mixture.

Put the bread on a large cookie sheet or baking pan, garlic-side up, and bake for 10 minutes, until lightly browned on top and heated all the way through. Please, oh please, oh please, don't leave the room while this is in the oven. In fact, don't answer the phone, don't read a book, don't do anything. A minute too long in the oven and the bread is, um, toast. Or worse.

Cut into chunks and serve warm.

# Guacamole

*This is the best thing to happen to a tortilla chip ever. Also* muy bien *with a taco or burrito and* excelente *with your quesadilla or nachos.*

2 large fully ripe avocados
1 small red onion, finely chopped
1 fresh jalapeño pepper, seeded and finely
   chopped
¼ cup (60 ml) chopped fresh cilantro
2 tbsp. (30 ml) fresh lime juice
½ tsp. (2 ml) salt

Cut the avocados in half, remove the pits and pull off the peel. If they're ripe, the peel will come off easily. Dice the avocado flesh and place it in a bowl. Add the onion, jalapeño, cilantro, lime juice and salt. Mash everything together gently — don't puree this; it should stay chunky. Taste, and adjust seasoning with a little more of this or that if you think it needs it.

Makes about 1 1/2 cups (375 ml) guacamole.

## Avocado magic!

Here's the easiest and cleanest way to dice an avocado. Cut the avocado in half, twist the two halves apart and remove the pit. Place one half on a cutting board and, with a sharp knife, cut criss-cross slices through the flesh just until the knife hits the peel (don't cut through). Once the flesh is cut, you can just spoon the cubes out of the shell directly into a bowl. Ta-da — no mess!

# Do-It-Yourself Dips

*Why on earth would you go out and buy a ready-made dip when making your own is such a snap? The following dips are divinely delicious and diabolically easy to devour. Definitely.*

## Dijon Dip

½ cup (125 ml) sour cream or plain Greek yogurt
¼ cup (60 ml) Dijon mustard
Salt, black pepper, hot pepper sauce, to taste

Stir everything together and serve with chips or pita crisps.

## Roasted Red Pepper and Feta Dip

1 cup (250 ml) crumbled feta cheese
1 roasted red pepper (from a jar), well drained and roughly chopped
1 tbsp. (15 ml) olive oil
1 clove garlic
¼ tsp. (1 ml) hot pepper flakes

Throw everything in the blender or food processor and whiz-z-z until smooth. Most excellent with pita bread but also great with veggie sticks.

## Homemade French Onion Dip

2 medium onions, chopped
2 tbsp. (30 ml) olive oil
¼ tsp. (1 ml) salt
1 cup (250 ml) sour cream
½ cup (125 ml) mayonnaise
Chopped green onion, and additional salt and pepper, if needed

Heat the olive oil in a skillet over medium heat. Add the onions and salt and cook, stirring occasionally, for about 30 minutes, or until the onions are a nice golden brown. Let cool to room temperature. Mix with the sour cream and mayonnaise, and chill for at least one hour. Stir in green onion and add salt and pepper, to taste.

# 7 Layer Taco Dip

*The ultimate expression of snackery as an art form. You can spread this out artistically on a large platter, with each layer peeking out from underneath the one on top of it. Or you can simply layer them in a baking dish. Doesn't matter. Irresistible.*

1 recipe Refried Beans (see page 152)
1 cup (250 ml) sour cream
1 cup (250 ml) prepared salsa, any kind — hot or not
1 cup (250 ml) shredded cheddar or Monterey Jack cheese
1 ripe avocado, peeled and diced
½ medium onion, chopped
¼ cup (60 ml) chopped fresh jalapeño peppers (or jalapeños from a jar, if you prefer)

On a large platter or in a 9 x 13-inch (23 x 33 cm) rectangular baking dish, spread the refried beans out in an even layer. Spoon the sour cream over the beans, and then spoon the salsa on top of the sour cream. They will blend together slightly — that's okay. Sprinkle with cheese, then avocado, onion and jalapeños.

Serve with plenty of tortilla chips.

# Hummus

*Better than store-bought, homemade takes no time to make. Go ahead — give it a whirl.*

1 can (19 oz./540 ml) chickpeas, drained (but save the liquid)
¼ cup (60 ml) tahini (sesame paste — available in most supermarkets and
   Middle Eastern grocery stores)
¼ cup (60 ml) lemon juice
2 cloves garlic
½ tsp. (2 ml) salt
½ tsp. (2 ml) ground cumin (optional)

In the container of a blender or food processor, combine the chickpeas, 1/4 cup (60 ml) of the chickpea liquid, tahini, lemon juice, garlic, salt and cumin (if using). Blend until really smooth, scraping down the sides of the blender several times with a rubber scraper. Hummus should be a little thicker than sour cream — if it's too thick, add a little more of the reserved chickpea liquid. Taste, and adjust the seasoning if necessary. Scoop into a bowl, sprinkle the top with a little chopped parsley and serve with fresh pita bread, pita crisps or raw vegetable dippers.

Makes about 2 cups (500 ml) hummus.

## Hummus gone wild!
**Roasted Red Pepper Hummus:** Add one jarred roasted red pepper to the blender with all the other ingredients and then top with some chopped roasted red pepper before serving.

**Hot and Spicy Hummus:** Toss a healthy dash of cayenne pepper and a fresh jalapeño pepper into the blender with everything else. Sprinkle the top with a little more cayenne.

**Sun-Dried Tomato and Basil Hummus:** Add ¼ cup (60 ml) oil-packed sun-dried tomatoes and 1 tbsp. (15 ml) fresh basil leaves when blending. Drizzle with a little of the oil from the jar of tomatoes.

**Olive Hummus:** Add ¼ cup (60 ml) pitted green, black or pimento-stuffed olives when blending. Top with a few chopped olives.

# Irresistible Maple Roasted Nuts

*Better than any mixed nuts you can buy, this is a killer snack to serve with drinks. Or pack the nuts into a fancy (recycled) jar, tie it up with a ribbon and give it as a gift to someone you really like. The bulk food store is your best friend here — just buy the quantity of nuts you need.*

1 cup (250 ml) whole almonds
1 cup (250 ml) walnut halves
1 cup (250 ml) pecan halves
1 cup (250 ml) whole hazelnuts
2 tbsp. (30 ml) olive oil
2 tbsp. (30 ml) pure maple syrup
1½ tsp. (7 ml) salt

Preheat the oven to 350°F (180°C). Lightly grease a cookie sheet or shallow baking pan with sides.

In a bowl, toss together all the nuts. Add the olive oil, maple syrup and salt, and mix until thoroughly and evenly coated. Transfer to the prepared cookie sheet. Place in the oven and bake for 20 to 25 minutes, stirring the nuts once or twice during the baking time. The nuts will still seem damp and sticky when you take them out of the oven, but they will become crisp once they cool. Let cool completely, then transfer to jars or a covered container for storage. As if they'll last that long.

Makes 4 cups (1 liter) nut mixture.

# Fake Escargots

*Escargots (in case you don't already know this) are snails. Regular, ordinary garden snails. Baked in garlic butter, they taste delicious. But so would a pencil eraser. Imagine, then, what that same garlic butter could do for a mushroom. With some crusty bread to soak up the sauce, this is a brilliant appetizer or snack.*

½ cup (125 ml) butter
2 tbsp. (30 ml) finely chopped onion
2 or 3 cloves garlic, minced or pressed
2 tbsp. (30 ml) finely chopped parsley
½ tsp. (2 ml) salt
¼ tsp. (1 ml) black pepper
24 medium mushrooms, rinsed, with stems removed

Preheat the oven to 375°F (190°C).

Melt the butter in a small saucepan over medium heat. Add the chopped onion, garlic and parsley. Stir in the salt and pepper, and remove from heat.

Arrange the mushrooms, gill-side up, in a baking dish just big enough to hold all of them in a single layer. Spoon the garlic butter over them, making sure the caps are filled. Place in the preheated oven and bake for 15 to 20 minutes, or until the mushrooms are tender. Serve hot, with some crusty French bread to soak up the garlicky butter sauce.

# Mushrooms Stuffed with Mushrooms

serves 6–8

*Make this with small or medium-size mushrooms and they're a perfect appetizer. Use this same recipe and stuff big, meaty portobello mushrooms instead and it's a very satisfying vegetarian main dish. Delicious either way.*

1 lb. (500 g) firm, fresh white or brown mushrooms
   (about twenty 2-inch/5 cm caps or 6 large portobello)
1 tbsp. (15 ml) olive oil or vegetable oil
1 medium onion, finely chopped
2 cloves garlic, minced or pressed
2 cups (500 ml) shredded sharp cheddar cheese
1 cup (250 ml) fresh bread crumbs
¼ cup (60 ml) chopped fresh parsley
½ tsp. (2 ml) salt
¼ tsp. (1 ml) black pepper
Additional oil for brushing mushrooms

Preheat the oven to 375°F (190°C). Grease a baking dish large enough to hold all the mushrooms without crowding.

Quickly rinse the mushrooms under running water and pat dry. Remove the stems from the caps and chop the stems as finely as you can manage. Lightly brush the mushroom caps with a little oil and arrange them in the baking dish.

Heat the oil in a small frying pan over medium-high heat. Add the chopped mushroom stems, onion and garlic, and cook, stirring often, for 6 to 8 minutes, until the onions are tender. Dump into a large bowl and add the cheese, bread crumbs, parsley, salt and pepper. Mix well.

Spoon the stuffing mixture into the caps, mounding them a little bit and pressing lightly so that the stuffing stays put. Bake in the preheated oven for 25 to 35 minutes, or until the mushrooms are sizzling and the stuffing is hot and lightly browned. (Large mushrooms will take longer to bake through than small ones.)

Makes 6 to 8 servings as an appetizer, 3 to 4 as a main dish.

# Deviled Eggs

*Always the first thing to disappear at a picnic or a potluck, devilled eggs are shockingly easy to make. Try the basic version first, then go crazy with some variations.*

6 eggs, hard boiled (see page 127) and peeled
2 tbsp. (30 ml) mayonnaise
1 tsp. (5 ml) Dijon mustard
¼ tsp. (1 ml) salt
Pinch black pepper
Paprika for sprinkling

Cut each egg in half lengthwise. Remove the egg yolks, as carefully as you can to avoid damaging the whites. Arrange the whites, cut-side up, on a plate.

Place the egg yolks in a bowl, and add the mayonnaise, mustard, salt and pepper. Mash with a fork until the mixture is creamy and smooth. Taste, and adjust seasoning if you think it needs more of something. Carefully spoon the yolk mixture into the egg whites and sprinkle with a little paprika for fun.

Makes 12 deviled egg halves.

## Devilishly delicious variations

**Wasabi Deviled Eggs:** Add 1 tsp. (5 ml) or more wasabi paste to the basic recipe. Sprinkle the eggs with sesame seeds (black ones look very snazzy).

**Guacamole Deviled Eggs:** Omit the mayonnaise in the basic recipe. Mash one ripe avocado and add to egg yolk mixture, along with a squeeze of lime juice and some finely chopped cilantro.

**Hot as Hell Deviled Eggs:** Add a dash of hot sauce (like Tabasco) to the basic mixture, along with one chopped jalapeño pepper. Sprinkle with cayenne, if you want to go all the way.

**Smoky Bacon Deviled Eggs:** Add ¼ tsp. (1 ml) smoked paprika to the basic recipe. Sprinkle the tops of the eggs with more smoked paprika and crumbled cooked bacon.

# The Smoothie Zone

*It's a cool and refreshing snack. It's a portable breakfast. It's lunch in a glass. Toss a bunch of stuff in the blender and see what happens. Bet it'll be delicious.*

## Breakfast Special

1 cup (250 ml) cold milk (regular or non-dairy)
½ cup (125 ml) plain or flavored yogurt
2 tbsp. (30 ml) orange juice concentrate (don't dilute it)
1 ripe banana, peeled and cut into chunks

Throw everything into the blender and let it zip while you tie your shoelaces. Quick — into a glass — and get going!

Makes about 2 cups (500 ml).

## Coconut Kale Craziness

½ cup (125 ml) coconut milk
½ cup (125 ml) pineapple juice or water
2 cups (500 ml) stemmed and torn kale (or spinach) leaves
1½ cups (375 ml) pineapple chunks (fresh, frozen or canned)
1 ripe banana, peeled and cut into chunks

Put the coconut milk, water, kale, pineapple and banana into the blender. Blend for at least one minute, until smooth, adding more water if needed.

Makes about 2 1/2 cups (625 ml).

## Peanut Berry Booster

¾ cup (175 ml) cold milk (regular or non-dairy)
¾ cup (175 ml) frozen strawberries or raspberries
½ ripe banana, peeled and cut into chunks
1 tbsp. (15 ml) peanut butter or almond butter
1 tbsp. (15 ml) honey, if desired

Put milk, berries, banana, peanut butter and honey (if using) into the blender. Blend until creamy and smooth.

Makes about 2 cups (500 ml).

## Mango Madness

1 cup (250 ml) cubed ripe mango, fresh or frozen
½ cup (125 ml) milk (regular or non-dairy)
½ cup (125 ml) ice
¼ cup (60 ml) plain yogurt
1 tbsp. (15 ml) honey, if desired

Buzz everything together in the blender until frothy and smooth.

Makes about 2 cups (500 ml).

A bowl of hot soup can help get you through a rough day. A fresh crisp salad can make you feel energized and virtuous. Either one can be served as part of a larger meal or be a whole meal on its own. And together — soup *and* salad — it's a classic combo. What's not to love?

# Soups and Salads

# Potato Soup

*A loaf of bread, a big bowl of potato soup — what more do you need? Okay, maybe a better apartment.*

2 medium onions, chopped
2 cloves garlic, minced or pressed
2 tbsp. (30 ml) butter, olive oil or vegetable oil
4 large potatoes, peeled and cubed (about 3 cups/750 ml cubed)
4 cups (1 liter) chicken broth or vegetable broth
    (prepared broth or made from bouillon cubes or powder)
2 cups (500 ml) milk
½ tsp. (2 ml) salt
¼ tsp. (1 ml) black pepper

In a large pot, sauté the onions and garlic in the butter or oil over medium heat for 3 to 5 minutes, or just until softened. Add the potatoes and the broth, and bring to a boil. Reduce the heat to medium low, cover the pot and simmer for 15 to 20 minutes, or until the potatoes are squishy and completely tender when poked with a fork. Let cool for a few minutes.

For a smooth and creamy soup, pour into a blender or food processor (do this in batches that will fit in your machine) and blend until smooth. Return to the pot. (If you have an immersion blender — sometimes called a stick blender — you can puree the soup right in the cooking pot.) Otherwise, for a more rustic look (but still delicious!) you can just mash the whole business with a fork or potato masher.

When your soup is pureed or mashed, add the milk, salt and pepper, place over medium-low heat and heat the soup through, stirring often, but don't let it boil.

## Cool French variation

Prepare the soup as above, then chill thoroughly. Serve cold, sprinkled with chopped chives or green onions, and call it vichyssoise. You may want to thin it with a bit of extra milk if the soup has thickened in the fridge. For extra bonus points, use 2 chopped leeks instead of the onions in the recipe.

# Sausage and Lentil Soup

*A full meal in a soup — in less than half an hour. You can do this.*

1 tbsp. (15 ml) olive oil or vegetable oil
1 medium onion, chopped
2 cloves garlic, minced or pressed
1 medium carrot, chopped
1 stalk celery, chopped
1 tsp. (5 ml) ground cumin
1 can (28 oz./796 ml) diced tomatoes
1 can (19 oz./540 ml) lentils, drained
2 cups (500 ml) chicken or vegetable broth
   (prepared broth or made from bouillon
   cubes
   or powder)
½ lb. (250 g) kielbasa or any smoked
   sausage
   cut into ½-inch (1 cm) cubes
½ tsp. (2 ml) salt
¼ tsp. (1 ml) black pepper

Heat the oil in a large saucepan or Dutch oven over medium heat, add the onion, garlic, carrot, celery and cumin, and cook, stirring once in a while, until the vegetables are soft and beginning to brown — about 10 minutes.

Add the diced tomatoes and all the juice in the can, then the lentils and the broth, and bring to a boil over medium-high heat. Reduce the heat to medium low, cover and let the soup simmer for about 15 minutes, or until the vegetables are tender. Add the sausage, salt and pepper, and continue to cook for another 5 minutes, or until heated through.

Serve with some good bread, and ta-da!

## Vegetarian alert!
Omit the sausage, use vegetable broth as the cooking liquid and double the lentils for a hearty vegetarian version of this soup.

# Classic Chicken Soup

*It started as a scratchy throat. Then you got a stuffy nose and a headache. And now — uh-oh — you're coughing. Make some chicken soup, wrap yourself in a blankie and eat your soup in front of the TV. Time to watch your favorite* Simpsons *episode. Again.*

5 lb. (2.5 kg) cheap chicken parts (necks, backs, legs, thighs, whatever is on sale)
1 large onion, chopped
4 stalks celery, cut in 1-inch/2 cm chunks
4 large carrots, peeled and cut in 1-inch/2 cm chunks
3 cloves garlic, peeled but left whole
1 handful fresh parsley leaves, washed
8 to 10 cups (2 to 2.5 liters) cold water (or enough to cover)
2 tsp. (10 ml) salt
½ tsp. (2 ml) black pepper

Rinse the chicken pieces under running water and put into a large pot. Add the onion, celery, carrots, garlic and parsley, and pour in enough cold water to cover everything with about 1 inch (2 cm) or so to spare. Bring to a boil over medium heat, then lower the heat to a simmer. Let cook, partly covered (leave the cover slightly ajar to prevent a boil-over), for at least 2 hours. Or longer, if you have the time.

Add the salt and pepper after the soup has been cooking for about 1 hour. At the end of the cooking time, taste the broth and adjust the seasoning. (If you have a cold, remember that your taste buds are shot, so have someone else do the tasting for you.)

Place a strainer or colander over another large pot and strain the soup completely. Let cool slightly, and with a large spoon skim as much of the fat (the clear, yellowish, floaty stuff) off the top as possible and discard it. (Neat trick: If you're not in a big hurry for your soup, refrigerate the broth overnight, then you can just scoop the congealed fat off the top easily.) Pick any meat off the bones, cut up the carrots and celery and throw these bits back into the broth. If you want noodles or rice (and who wouldn't?), cook them separately in boiling water until tender before adding to the chicken soup.

There you go. Chicken soup that will make you feel much better if you're sick but can also be safely consumed by a perfectly healthy person.

Makes about 2 quarts (2 liters).

# Split Pea Soup

*Quicker and easier to make than you would think. And vegetarian too! Amazing.*

2 cups (500 ml) dry split peas (green or yellow, it doesn't matter)
8 cups (2 liters) cold water
2 stalks celery, chopped
2 medium carrots, chopped
2 medium onions, chopped
1 tsp. (5 ml) salt
½ tsp. (2 ml) black pepper
2 tbsp. (30 ml) chopped fresh parsley

Rinse the split peas in several changes of water and then place them in a large pot or Dutch oven. Add the cold water and bring to a boil over medium-high heat. Reduce the heat to low, cover the pot and simmer for about 20 minutes, stirring occasionally, until the peas are soft.

Add the celery, carrots, onions, salt, pepper and parsley. Bring the soup to a boil over medium-high heat, and then reduce the heat to low and simmer, covered, for another 30 minutes, until the vegetables are tender and the split peas have almost completely disintegrated.

Taste, and adjust seasoning if necessary.

## Ham it up!

Traditionally, split pea soup is made with ham. So if you happen to *not* be a vegetarian, and you miss that smoky, meaty flavor, go ahead and add some chopped cooked ham to the soup along with the celery and carrots.

## Garbage Broth — It's free!

Celery leaves. Parsley stems. Green pepper insides. Chicken bones. Rubbery carrots. Meat trimmings. You weren't planning to throw that stuff away, were you? Of course not. What looks like garbage to the untrained eye is actually the makings of a flavorful broth. Just toss all these bits and pieces — vegetable trimmings, wilted leaves, cores, stems — into a plastic bag in the freezer. When you've saved up enough of this junk to fill a pot, add water to cover, and simmer until the cows come home. You may have to throw in some extra seasonings for flavor — salt, pepper, herbs, spices — but eventually your concoction will turn into something broth-y and worthwhile. Strain out the solids and use it as a base for soup.

# Roasted Carrot Soup

serves 4–6

*This is the best carrot soup you've ever tasted. Roasting the carrots brings out the amazingness in this seemingly ordinary vegetable.*

1½ lb. (750 g) medium carrots, scrubbed or peeled, cut into 2-inch (5 cm) chunks — about 8 medium carrots
3 tbsp. (45 ml) olive oil, divided
½ tsp. (2 ml) salt
¼ tsp. (1 ml) black pepper
2 medium onions, chopped
1 tbsp. (15 ml) finely grated fresh ginger
4 cups (1 liter) chicken broth or vegetable broth (prepared broth or made from bouillon cubes or powder)
½ cup (125 ml) whipping cream

Preheat the oven to 400°F (200°C). Have ready a rimmed cookie sheet.

Place the carrots in a mixing bowl. Add 2 tbsp. (30 ml) of the olive oil, the salt and pepper, and toss until the carrots are coated. Dump into the cookie sheet and spread the carrots out in a single layer.

Place in the oven and bake for 40 to 45 minutes, or until the carrots are tender and beginning to brown. Mix them around 2 or 3 times as they roast. Remove from the oven and set aside.

In a large saucepan, cook the onions in the remaining 1 tbsp. (15 ml) of olive oil, stirring occasionally, until golden, about 6 to 8 minutes. Add the roasted carrots, ginger and broth, and bring to a boil over medium heat. Lower the heat slightly, cover the saucepan and simmer for about 10 minutes. Let cool slightly.

Working in 2 or 3 batches, pour the soup into the container of a blender and blend the heck out of it, until completely smooth. (If you have an immersion blender, you can do this right in the pot, thus saving some extra dishwashing.) Return the blended soup to the pot, add the whipping cream and place over medium heat just until heated through. Taste, and adjust the seasoning with salt and pepper if you think it needs it.

## Veganize it!
Use vegetable broth as the base for this soup and substitute canned coconut milk for the whipping cream. Bingo — it's vegan!

# Mushroom Barley Soup

*An old-fashioned homey soup that's perfect for a stormy day when you need a little comfort food.*

2 tbsp. (30 ml) butter, olive oil or vegetable oil

2 medium onions, chopped

2 medium carrots, chopped

1 stalk celery, chopped

2 cloves garlic, minced or pressed

1 lb. (500 g) mushrooms, trimmed and sliced

3 quarts (3 liters) chicken or vegetable broth (prepared broth or made
   from bouillon cubes or powder)

½ cup (125 ml) uncooked pearl barley

1 tsp. (5 ml) dried thyme

1 tsp. (5 ml) salt

¼ tsp. (1 ml) black pepper

2 tbsp. (30 ml) chopped fresh parsley

In a large pot, heat the butter or oil over medium heat. Add the onions, carrots, celery and garlic, and cook, stirring, for about 10 minutes, or until the vegetables are beginning to get tender. Add the sliced mushrooms and let cook for another 5 to 8 minutes, or until the mushrooms have released their juices (wait for it!), then cook, stirring, for 2 or 3 minutes longer.

Now add the broth, barley, thyme, salt and pepper, and bring to a boil over medium-high heat. Cover the pot with a lid, lower the heat to medium low and let the soup cook, stirring occasionally, for about 1 hour, or until the barley is completely tender. If the soup is becoming too thick, add a bit more broth (or even just water) to thin it. Add the chopped parsley and simmer for another 5 to 10 minutes.

# Minestrone Soup

serves 10

*Old minestrone secret: If you grate your own Parmesan cheese, save the rinds and toss a couple of hunks into the soup as it cooks to add some serious flavor. Fish them out of the pot before serving.*

2 tbsp. (30 ml) olive oil or vegetable oil
2 medium onions, chopped
2 cloves garlic, minced or pressed
1 carrot, sliced ¼-inch (.5 cm) thick
2 stalks celery, sliced ¼-inch (.5 cm) thick
1 can (28 oz./796 ml) diced tomatoes
4 cups (1 liter) water
½ cup (125 ml) any small pasta shape, uncooked (like small shells or tubes)
1 cup (250 ml) green beans, cut crosswise into ½-inch (1 cm) pieces
2 small zucchini, sliced ¼-inch (.5 cm) thick
3 cups (750 ml) raw spinach, roughly torn up
1 can (19 oz./540 ml) red or white kidney beans, rinsed and drained
½ tsp. (2 ml) salt
¼ tsp. (1 ml) black pepper
Grated Parmesan cheese for serving, if desired

Before you begin, take some time to chop, dice and slice all the ingredients for the soup. Once you start cooking, you'll be glad it's all ready to go.

Heat the oil in a large pot over medium heat. Add the onions and garlic, and sauté for about 5 minutes, or until softened. Add the carrots, celery, tomatoes and water. (If you have any Parmesan cheese rinds, add them now.) Bring to a boil, then reduce the heat to low, cover the pot and simmer, stirring occasionally, for about 40 minutes — just long enough to clean up the mess in the kitchen. Almost.

Now add the uncooked pasta and the green beans, and cook for 10 minutes. Finally, add the zucchini, spinach and canned beans, and continue to cook for another 10 to 20 minutes. Season with salt and pepper.

Pass around grated Parmesan cheese at the table to sprinkle on each serving, if desired.

# Gazpacho                                                          serves 6

*Look! In your bowl! Is it a soup? Is it salad? On a hot summer day, who really cares? Make sure to use flavorful, in-season tomatoes for this.*

3 cloves garlic, minced or pressed
4 ripe tomatoes
4 cups (1 liter) tomato juice or tomato-vegetable juice, divided
6 green onions, cut into chunks
2 stalks celery, cut into chunks
2 medium cucumbers, peeled and diced
1 sweet green or red pepper, seeded and diced
1 small fresh hot pepper (very optional)
¼ cup (60 ml) lemon juice
1 tsp. (5 ml) salt
¼ tsp. (1 ml) black pepper
Sour cream or plain Greek yogurt for serving, if desired
Finely chopped parsley or chives for serving, if desired

In the container of a blender or food processor, combine the garlic, 2 of the tomatoes and about half the tomato juice, and blend until smooth. Add the green onions, celery, cucumbers, sweet pepper and hot pepper, and blend — with quick on/off pulses — just so the vegetables are coarsely chopped. This mixture should stay quite chunky. Transfer gazpacho to a large mixing bowl. Stir in the remaining tomato juice, lemon juice, salt and pepper. Chop the remaining 2 tomatoes coarsely and add to the soup. Taste, and adjust seasoning with more salt and pepper if you think it needs it. Chill for at least 1 hour, if possible.

To serve, ladle the gazpacho into bowls, swirl in a small blob of sour cream or yogurt and sprinkle with parsley or chives. Or just serve it plain. Either way, it's great.

# Corn Chowder

*Chunky, corny and easy — you can make this soup with fresh corn when it's in season or with frozen corn in the winter.*

2 tbsp. (30 ml) butter, olive oil or vegetable oil
2 medium onions, chopped
2 medium potatoes, peeled and cut into ½-inch (1 cm) cubes
4 cups (1 liter) chicken or vegetable broth (prepared broth or made from
    bouillon cubes or powder)
2 cups (500 ml) milk
1 tsp. (5 ml) salt
¼ tsp. (1 ml) black pepper
4 cups (1 liter) corn kernels (frozen or cut from 5 or 6 fresh cobs)
2 tbsp. (30 ml) chopped fresh parsley

Heat the butter or oil in a large pot or Dutch oven over medium heat. Add the onions and cook, stirring frequently, for 5 to 7 minutes, until softened. Add the potatoes, broth, milk, salt and pepper. Bring to a boil, then reduce the heat to medium low, cover and let simmer for 10 to 15 minutes, until the potatoes are almost tender.

Stir in the corn kernels and cook for 10 more minutes, until the corn is tender and the potatoes are very soft.

Remove about 2 cups (500 ml) of the soup and put it into the container of a blender or food processor. Blend until smooth, then return it to the rest of the soup in the pot. Stir in the chopped parsley and heat through.

# Chunky Pasta Salad

serves 4–6

*Pasta salad was invented to take care of leftovers. A bit of cooked pasta, some slivers of red pepper, a few cooked green beans, half an onion, a forgotten hunk of cheese — that sort of thing. Throw it all into a bowl, add some dressing and you've made something out of nothing.*

2 cups (500 ml) uncooked rotini or shells or other medium-size pasta shape (or 3 cups/750 ml cooked pasta)
1 tsp. (5 ml) olive oil or vegetable oil
3 cups (750 ml) total amount mixed diced cooked and raw vegetables, cheese, ham, chicken breast, salami, canned beans or chickpeas
¼ cup (60 ml) mayonnaise
¼ cup (60 ml) plain yogurt
2 tsp. (10 ml) apple cider vinegar or white wine vinegar
1 clove garlic, minced or pressed
½ tsp. (2 ml) salt
¼ tsp. (1 ml) black pepper

If you're starting with uncooked pasta, bring a large pot of salted water to a boil. Add the pasta, and cook on high heat until the pasta is tender but not at all mushy. Drain in a colander, then rinse under cold running water. Place in a large bowl and toss with the oil to keep the pasta from sticking together. If you're using leftover cooked pasta, just rinse with cold water to remove surface starch, then toss in a bowl with the oil.

Add all the vegetables and whatever other chunky bits you're putting in the salad (the chicken, cheese, beans and so on). If you're not serving the salad right away, cover with plastic wrap and refrigerate until ready to serve.

In a small bowl, whisk together the mayonnaise, yogurt, vinegar, garlic, salt and pepper. Just before serving, combine the salad with the dressing and toss so that everything is evenly mixed. Don't add the dressing more than half an hour before you want to eat, because the pasta will soak it up like a sponge. (You can make the salad and dressing ahead of time, but keep them separate until you're ready to serve.) Taste, and adjust the seasoning, if necessary.

If there's any salad left over, refrigerate it and toss with additional dressing just before serving.

## How to make a simple tossed salad

1. Begin with lettuce. Try several kinds, if you're feeling bold — or just the kind you like best. Buy a package of mixed baby greens, or some romaine hearts, or a big old head of iceberg.
2. Add some other things: escarole, endive, radicchio, arugula. Be brave. What could possibly go wrong? They're only leaves.
3. Rinse and dry everything well — use a salad spinner if you have one.
4. Now add stuff. Tomato chunks, cucumber slices, shredded carrot, red pepper, red onion, red cabbage, radishes, whatever. Or be a purist and add nothing at all. Your choice.
5. Drizzle with just enough homemade dressing, whatever kind you like (see pages 48 through 52), to lightly coat the leaves. Toss gently and serve immediately.
6. There. Simple, isn't it?

# Perfect Potato Salad                    serves 4

*Even better than your mom's. But don't tell her that.*

4 or 5 medium potatoes, peeled and cut into ½-inch (1 cm) cubes
2 tbsp. (30 ml) apple cider vinegar or white wine vinegar
2 tbsp. (30 ml) water
½ tsp. (2 ml) salt
¼ tsp. (1 ml) black pepper
1 small onion, chopped
1 stalk celery, diced
1 or 2 hard-boiled eggs, peeled and chopped (see page 127)
½ cup (125 ml) mayonnaise
2 tbsp. (30 ml) chopped fresh parsley

First, cook your potatoes. Place the cubed potatoes in a steamer basket over boiling water and cook until you can poke a fork into them without resistance (be careful not to overcook or they'll fall apart). This shouldn't take more than about 15 minutes. If you prefer, you can boil the potatoes in a medium saucepan of boiling water for the same amount of time. Transfer the cooked potatoes to a medium-size bowl.

In a small bowl, mix together the vinegar, water, salt and pepper. Toss with the warm potatoes, being careful not to mush them up. Refrigerate until completely cool.

When the potatoes are cool, add the onion, celery, eggs, mayonnaise and parsley — and toss until everything is well mixed. Chill thoroughly before serving.

# Crunchy Cucumber Salad

serves 3–4

*When lettuce is $4 a head and tomatoes are tough as tennis balls, you can still have salad with dinner.*

2 seedless English cucumbers, peeled
   (if you like) and thinly sliced
2 tsp. (10 ml) salt
¼ cup (60 ml) white vinegar
2 tsp. (10 ml) granulated sugar
¼ to ½ cup (60 to 125 ml) sour cream,
   if desired
Black pepper, to taste

> **Fancy it up!**
> Want to give your cucumber salad a bit of a makeover? Try this: Without peeling the cucumbers, run a fork lengthwise all the way down the sides, all the way around. Now slice thinly. Look! Scalloped edges! Aren't you brilliant?

In a medium bowl, toss the cucumber slices with the 2 tsp. (10 ml) salt. Let this sit for about 30 minutes to allow the salt to draw the excess water out of the cucumber. Drain as much of the water off as possible and return cucumbers to the bowl.

Add the vinegar and sugar to the drained cucumbers, and toss. If you want a creamy dressing, stir in 1/4 to 1/2 cup (60 to 125 ml) sour cream (but it's good without the sour cream too). Add a sprinkle of black pepper if you like.

Serve immediately.

# Authentic Greek Salad

serves 4–6

*This salad is best in midsummer, when it can be made with perfectly ripe, in-season tomatoes that actually taste like, well, tomatoes. You can easily make a full meal out of it with the addition of some good bread and a little extra cheese. Or you can stuff it into the pocket of a pita bread and have it for lunch on the run.*

4 medium tomatoes, cut into ½-inch (1 cm) chunks
1 seedless English cucumber, cut into ½-inch (1 cm) chunks
1 small red onion, diced
⅓ cup (75 ml) Zorba the Greek Dressing (see recipe on page 51)
4 oz. (125 g) feta cheese, crumbled (about 1 cup/250 ml)
½ cup (125 ml) black olives (kalamata or other brine-cured ones are best)
Salt and black pepper, to taste

In a large bowl, toss together the tomatoes, cucumber and onion.

Add the dressing and toss to mix. Sprinkle in the feta cheese and olives, and toss gently.

Taste the salad, adjust the seasoning with additional salt and pepper if you think it needs it and serve immediately.

# Coleslaw

*The world's cheapest and easiest salad. Toss it with Sweet and Sour Dressing (see page 52) if you want it to last for a few days in the fridge. Coleslaw with a creamy dressing (see page 51) should be eaten soon after it's made. Creamy dressing goes especially well with coleslaw that includes ingredients like apples and raisins — but you'll have it your own way, won't you?*

½ small head of cabbage, shredded or very finely sliced (about 6 cups/1½
    liters)
2 green onions, chopped
1 carrot, grated
1 green pepper, chopped
1 apple, chopped (optional)
½ cup (125 ml) raisins (optional)
1 recipe Sweet and Sour Coleslaw Dressing (see recipe on page 52) *or*
    Creamy Coleslaw Dressing (see recipe on page 51)

In a large bowl, combine all the shredded and chopped ingredients and toss well.

Add whichever dressing you're using and toss again until everything is coated.

# Citrus Spinach Salad

*Use tender baby spinach leaves to make this gorgeous salad. So good.*

2 pkg. (10 oz./284 g) baby spinach leaves (about 6 cups/1.5 liters loose leaves)
1 seedless orange, peeled, sectioned and cut into chunks
½ small sweet onion (red onion or Vidalia is nice), thinly sliced
¼ cup (60 ml) Basic Vinaigrette Dressing (see recipe on page 48)

In a large bowl, toss together the spinach, orange chunks and onion slices.

Drizzle with Basic Vinaigrette Dressing and toss well. Gorgeous.

## Got strawberries?

When they're in season, substitute sliced or halved fresh strawberries for the orange in this salad. Ta-da! Strawberry Spinach Salad. So pretty and delicious. Sprinkle chopped or sliced toasted almonds over the top for extra crunch.

# Spicy Asian Asparagus Salad

serves 4

*An asparagus flavor bomb — addictive with a kick.*

1½ lb. (750 ml) fresh asparagus, trimmed and cut into 2-inch (5 cm) pieces
2 tbsp. (30 ml) granulated sugar
2 tbsp. (30 ml) cider vinegar or rice vinegar
2 tbsp. (30 ml) sesame oil
1 tbsp. (15 ml) Asian chili paste (see below)
1 tsp. (5 ml) salt
2 tbsp. (30 ml) vegetable oil
6 cloves garlic, cut into slivers

Place the asparagus pieces in a steamer basket over boiling water and steam for 2 to 3 minutes, just until asparagus turns bright green. Watch carefully to avoid overcooking.

Dump the asparagus into a strainer and run cold water over it to stop it from cooking further. Let drain.

In a small bowl, combine the sugar, vinegar, sesame oil, chili paste and salt. Set aside.

In a wok or large skillet, heat the vegetable oil over high heat. Add the slivered garlic, stir for no more than 1 minute, then add the chili paste mixture and stir to mix. Remove from heat.

Stir the asparagus into the sauce mixture and toss to combine. Cover and chill before serving. If you can wait that long.

## Asian chili paste

Spicy and intense, Asian chili paste comes in many different varieties — some with garlic, some with black beans, some chunky and some smooth. You can usually find it in the Asian section of a large supermarket — to make this salad, use whichever type you can find. Sriracha sauce will do nicely if that's what is available, but go ahead and experiment with different types if you want. It's a great big spicy world out there.

# Tabbouleh Salad

*A Middle Eastern classic. Serve it as is as part of a meal, or add some cooked chicken or a can of chickpeas and call it dinner.*

1 cup (250 ml) bulgur
2 cups (500 ml) boiling water
3 medium tomatoes, diced
1 medium cucumber, diced
1 bunch fresh parsley, chopped
¼ cup (60 ml) olive oil
2 tbsp. (30 ml) lemon juice
1 clove garlic, minced or pressed
½ tsp. (2 ml) salt
¼ tsp. (1 ml) black pepper

Place the bulgur in a large mixing bowl, then add the boiling water and stir. Cover and let sit for at least 15 minutes — the bulgur should absorb all the water and become tender but still remain a bit chewy.

Line a strainer or colander with a clean dish towel. Dump the bulgur into the towel, then lift it out and twist the whole business to wring as much of the excess water out of the bulgur as possible. I know — this seems weird. Transfer to a large bowl — the bulgur should be fluffy and not at all soggy.

Add the tomatoes, cucumber and parsley, and toss to mix.

In a small bowl, whisk together the olive oil, lemon juice, garlic, salt and pepper. Drizzle this dressing over the bulgur and vegetables in the bowl, and toss everything to mix well.

## Couscous tabbouleh is a real thing!

Cook 1 cup (250 ml) of couscous according to the recipe on page 149. Use instead of the bulgur wheat for a couscous version of this very same salad.

# Multibean Salad

*Colorful, tasty and cheap! Any leftovers will keep for several days, refrigerated.*

3 cans (19 oz./540 ml each) red or white kidney beans, chickpeas,
   black beans or mixed beans
1 medium yellow or red onion, diced
1 medium sweet green, red or yellow pepper, diced
1 medium tomato, diced (or 1 cup/250 ml cherry or grape tomatoes, halved)
¼ cup (60 ml) chopped fresh parsley
½ cup (125 ml) olive oil or vegetable oil
⅓ cup (75 ml) apple cider vinegar, balsamic vinegar or other vinegar
1 clove garlic, minced or pressed
2 tbsp. (30 ml) granulated sugar
1 tsp. (5 ml) salt
½ tsp. (2 ml) black pepper

Open the cans of beans and dump them into a colander. Rinse under cold running water, drain well and transfer to a large mixing bowl. Add the onion, sweet pepper, tomato and parsley.

In a small bowl, whisk together the oil, vinegar, garlic, sugar, salt and black pepper. Pour this dressing over the bean mixture and toss well to mix. Cover with plastic wrap and chill in the refrigerator for about 1 hour to let the ingredients get to know one another. Just before serving, toss again to mix.

### Great antipasto

Antipasto is a work of art. A symphony. Well, maybe that's a little much. But anyway, it's not meat loaf — although there could be meat loaf in it. Or practically anything else, for that matter. It can consist of three or four well-chosen and delicious items arranged on a plate or it can be a wild collection of odds and ends. It can be an appetizer or it can be dinner. And the nicest thing about it is that you don't actually have to cook anything.

Some of the following items can be found at an Italian grocery store; some you can pick up from your supermarket deli. Some things are fresh and others come out of cans or jars. Use your imagination — express yourself in your antipasto.

- marinated artichoke hearts
- sliced provolone, Swiss or Asiago cheese
- canned anchovies or sardines
- olives — green, black, wrinkled, spicy, stuffed or plain
- thinly sliced Italian salami, ham or prosciutto
- bocconcini (little fresh mozzarella cheese balls)
- pickled peppers
- marinated mushrooms
- cherry tomatoes
- roasted red peppers or eggplant
- sun-dried tomatoes (oil-packed with herbs)
- canned tuna
- hard-boiled egg wedges
- celery and carrot sticks

Arrange your chosen antipasto components decoratively on a platter — roll up the cheese and sliced meat, make a face with the olives, garnish everything with a pickled pepper — you know the sort of thing.

Serve with a warm loaf of crusty Italian or French bread (if you happen to find fresh focaccia or ciabatta, grab it).

*Buon appetito!*

# Spectacular Salad Dressings

Step away from the bottle. You can (and should) make your own salad dressing. It costs next to nothing, takes about 5 minutes to mix and will be better tasting and fresher than anything you can buy in the store.

## Basic Vinaigrette Dressing

*Use this no-nonsense dressing as it is or bling it up with extra ingredients and see what happens. Use olive oil if you have it in the house and whatever vinegar you want (see lists opposite). Experiment with different oils and vinegars and see how one basic dressing can go in so many different directions. Add fresh*

*or dried herbs, spices, grated cheese, garlic, ketchup —*
*mess around and see what you can come up with.*

¾ cup (175 ml) olive oil (or see other options, sidebar)
¼ cup (60 ml) vinegar of your choice (see sidebar)
1 tbsp. (15 ml) Dijon mustard
½ tsp. (2 ml) salt
¼ tsp. (1 ml) black pepper

In a small bowl, whisk all the ingredients together until
thoroughly mixed. Taste, and adjust salt and pepper, if
needed. The Dijon mustard in the recipe will help keep
the dressing mixed for a while (technically speaking,
emulsified), but it will still eventually separate. No big
deal — just re-whisk if necessary.

Makes about 1 cup (250 ml) — enough for at least a
couple of big salads. Leftover dressing keeps practically
forever in the fridge.

## Creamy Italian Dressing
*Start with Basic Vinaigrette Dressing (above), then add a*
*few things and turn it into Creamy Italian. Just like that.*

1 recipe Basic Vinaigrette Dressing, preferably made
    with olive oil (see page 48)
¼ cup (60 ml) mayonnaise
1 clove garlic, pressed
½ tsp. (2 ml) crumbled dried oregano
¼ tsp. (1 ml) crumbled dried thyme
Additional salt and black pepper, to taste

In a small bowl, whisk the ingredients together until thoroughly mixed. Taste,
and adjust seasoning, if necessary.

Makes about 1 cup (250 ml).

## Somewhat Caesar Dressing
*Another Basic Vinaigrette variation. See — isn't it useful?*

1 recipe Basic Vinaigrette Dressing (see page 48)
¼ cup (60 ml) mayonnaise
1 clove garlic, minced or pressed (or more, if you like)

## Oil options
- avocado oil
- canola oil
- corn oil
- grape seed oil
- olive oil
- peanut oil
- sesame oil
- sunflower oil
- vegetable oil
  (usually soy)
- walnut oil

## Vinegar variations
- apple cider
  vinegar
- red or white
  balsamic
  vinegar
- red or white
  wine vinegar
- rice vinegar
- sherry vinegar
- white vinegar
- lemon juice

1 tsp. (5 ml) Worcestershire sauce
2 tbsp. (30 ml) grated Parmesan cheese (or more, to taste)
1 or 2 canned anchovies, minced (a classic touch, but optional)
Additional salt and pepper, to taste

Whisk the Basic Vinaigrette Dressing and the mayonnaise until well mixed. Add the garlic, Worcestershire sauce, Parmesan cheese and anchovies (if you're using them). Whisk again until smooth. Taste, and adjust with additional salt and pepper if you think it needs it.

Makes a little more than 1 cup (250 ml). Leftover dressing can be refrigerated for 2 or 3 days.

## Desperation Ranch Dressing

*Desperation is, after all, the mother of invention.*

½ cup (125 ml) mayonnaise
¼ cup (60 ml) dill pickle juice
Additional salt and black pepper, to taste

Mix the mayonnaise and the pickle juice, adjusting the seasoning with salt and pepper (and maybe garlic) until the dressing tastes right. You can use the juice from any kind of pickle for this recipe if you don't happen to have dill pickles in the house.

Makes 3/4 cup (175 ml) — enough for a couple of big salads. Leftover dressing keeps well in the fridge.

### How to chop an onion without crying

Amaze your friends and family with this spectacular trick! Place your cutting board over the front burner of the stove. (Do not turn it on!) Pay attention here — this is critical — turn the *back burner* on high. The back burner gets turned on — *the front burner is off.* Got that? Now place your onion on the cutting board (which is sitting on the *front* burner, which *is not turned on*) and chop away to your heart's content. For complex scientific reasons, the heat from the back burner of the stove attracts the tear-producing onion vapors and draws them away from your delicate eyeballs. Unbelievable but true. Just please don't forget to turn that stove burner off when you're finished chopping. And, of course, take a bow. Ta-da!

A scuba mask also works — but isn't quite as awesome.

## What is a garlic clove — and how do you chop it?

When a recipe calls for a clove of garlic, it means *one section* of the bulb. If the recipe calls for a head of garlic (we're talking serious garlic here), you'll be using the *whole bulb* (this doesn't happen very often).

Some recipes ask you to *chop*, *mince* or *press* a clove of garlic. Here's a quick, violent method to do the job: Place the clove on a chopping board, yell "HAYAH!" and whack the garlic with the side of a broad knife. The skin will peel off and the garlic clove will be mostly in pieces. Remove the bits of peel. A few additional chops and you now have chopped garlic. More chopping and you will have minced garlic (smaller bits). Very effective — and fun.

For pressed garlic, use a garlic press. Simple!

## Zorba the Greek Dressing

*Mandatory on an Authentic Greek Salad (see recipe on page 42). Singing, dancing and plate smashing are optional (but fun).*

½ cup (125 ml) olive oil
3 tbsp. (45 ml) lemon juice
1 tsp. (5 ml) crumbled dried oregano
½ tsp. (2 ml) salt
¼ tsp. (1 ml) black pepper

In a small bowl, whisk together all the ingredients until combined.

Makes 3/4 cup (175 ml) dressing — enough for a couple of bowls of Greek salad. You can keep any leftover dressing in the fridge for about a week.

## Creamy Coleslaw Dressing

*Substitute plain Greek yogurt for up to half of the mayonnaise, if you prefer. The flavor will be a little different, but it will still be creamy and delicious.*

¾ cup (175 ml) mayonnaise
¼ cup (60 ml) apple cider vinegar
2 tbsp. (30 ml) granulated sugar
1 tbsp. (15 ml) Dijon mustard
½ tsp. (2 ml) salt
¼ tsp. (1 ml) black pepper

In a small bowl, mix together all the ingredients until blended.

Makes 1 cup (250 ml) dressing — enough for a very large bowl of coleslaw. Leftover dressing keeps well in the refrigerator.

# Sweet and Sour Coleslaw Dressing

*Coleslaw made with this type of dressing will keep very nicely in the fridge for several days. If anything, it's actually better the next day.*

½ cup (125 ml) vegetable oil (sunflower or other neutral oil is good)
⅓ cup (75 ml) apple cider vinegar
1 tbsp. (15 ml) granulated sugar
1 tsp. (5 ml) celery seeds
1 tsp. (5 ml) salt
¼ tsp. (1 ml) black pepper

Whisk all the ingredients together in a small bowl.

Makes about 1 cup (250 ml) dressing — enough for a large bowl of coleslaw. Any leftover dressing keeps well.

# Balsamic Garlic Dressing

*Here's another great basic dressing that you can keep around the house. It goes best with sturdy greens (romaine, arugula, kale) and keeps well, refrigerated, for several days.*

1 cup (250 ml) olive oil
¼ cup (60 ml) balsamic vinegar
2 cloves garlic, chopped
1 tbsp. (15 ml) Dijon mustard
1 tsp. (5 ml) salt
½ tsp. (2 ml) black pepper

Combine all the ingredients in a blender and blend until creamy.

Makes about 1 1/2 cups (375 ml) dressing. Leftovers will keep in the refrigerator for several days. If the dressing separates, just whisk it a bit to re-combine before using.

# Mainly Meat

## How to Buy Meat

Meat is scary. It comes with no cooking instructions, it all looks identical and the same chunk of meat may have several different names. That's almost enough to turn a person into a vegetarian. Or not.

**Make friends with a butcher.** Ask stupid questions: What is this? What do you do with it? Is it any good? Most butchers are only too happy to share pearls of carnivorous wisdom with anyone who is interested. An especially enthusiastic butcher may even divulge a favorite recipe.

**The ground beef dilemma.** Ground chuck? Ground sirloin? Ground round? Twenty percent fat? Fifteen percent fat? Thirty percent fat? Such a basic food item — how do you decide what to buy? Generally, the higher the percentage of fat, the less expensive the meat; the leaner the meat, the more expensive it will be. Buy lean or extra-lean ground beef (10 percent fat or less) when you're making something like meat loaf — where the fat doesn't really get a chance to drain off. You can get away with cheaper regular ground beef (up to 30 percent fat) if you're making chili or spaghetti sauce — where you can drain the excess fat after browning. A good compromise for most purposes — like making an actual hamburger — is medium ground beef with 15 to 20 percent fat. Many supermarkets mark their ground beef with these percentages to help

### A brief compendium of meat, or Help! How do you cook this thing?

**Fire up the barbecue**
- beef rib and rib eye steak
- beef strip loin or New York steak
- beef tenderloin or filet mignon
- beef sirloin
- beef flank steak
- any ground meat
- sausages and hot dogs
- lamb chops
- pork rib or loin chops
- pork tenderloin
- pork spare ribs
- ham steak
- chicken, whole or parts
- turkey breast cutlets

**Tender and roast-worthy**
- beef rib roast
- beef sirloin roast
- beef top round or eye of round roast
- beef tenderloin
- pork loin
- pork leg or ham
- lamb leg or shoulder
- chicken
- turkey
- duck

**Slow and steady — stew, pot roast or braise with liquid**
- beef chuck, blade or shoulder
- beef bottom round
- beef brisket
- beef short ribs
- beef stewing meat
- pork shoulder roast or chops
- lamb shoulder or stewing lamb
- chicken
- turkey thighs

you choose; others will simply label ground beef as regular, medium, lean or extra lean.

**What about ground turkey, chicken, lamb and pork?** Go ahead and try them instead of ground beef in your favorite recipe. The taste and texture will be different, but your substitution will work — you may even like your variation better.

**No, sausages are not made from ground-up rats.** Meat safety regulations are extremely strict. So unless you buy sausages from some guy named Igor who lives down the street and makes them in his basement, you can be sure they're safe as long as the meat has been properly handled and cooked.

**Most big chunks of meat look alike.** But they aren't alike. If you don't know what you want to make, buy meat that's on sale and ask the butcher (or your mom) how to cook it. If you have a specific dish in mind, find out which cut of meat is appropriate. Either way, you'll have to do some homework.

**Not all steaks are created equal.** Only a select few types of steak are tender enough to slap on the grill just the way they are. Others need to be marinated before cooking. Still others should be gently simmered in some stew-y concoction.

**Rule of thumb:** Meat from the hind end of the animal is more tender than meat from the front. Learn your animal anatomy by consulting a meat chart or asking the butcher.

# A Perfect Hamburger

*Perfection, hamburger-wise, is in the mouth of the beholder. Some people like to add a lot of stuff to their burger mixture; others like to put lots of stuff on top after cooking. Here's a basic recipe that you can mess with until you've found your own personal burger nirvana.*

1 lb. (500 g) lean ground beef
¼ cup (60 ml) water (yes, water — it keeps the meat moist)
2 tbsp. (30 ml) soy sauce (if you have it)
½ tsp. (2 ml) salt
¼ tsp. (1 ml) black pepper
Vegetable oil for greasing skillet, if cooking stovetop

In a bowl, with a fork or bare-handed, mix the ground beef with the water, soy sauce, salt and pepper. Don't mush it to death — the secret of a perfect burger is not to handle the meat too much. Whenever you're working with meat, remember to sanitize all surfaces (and your hands!) after you're finished to prevent any cross-contamination.

With a light touch, form the meat mixture into 3 or 4 patties, squishing them just enough so they don't fall apart. Flatten the burgers to an even thickness — around 1/2 inch (1 cm) is good. (Your burgers will shrink a bit as they cook.) Place on a plate, cover and refrigerate until you're ready to cook them.

If you're using a barbecue grill or oven broiler, preheat it to medium high. If you're cooking your burgers on a skillet, lightly grease the skillet with vegetable oil and place it over medium-high heat.

Whichever method you're using, cook your burgers until they're evenly browned on both sides, flipping them once or twice, until they're no longer pink in the middle (cut into one to check). If your heat is too high, the outsides of the burgers may burn before the insides are done — reduce the heat so they cook through without becoming incinerated.

Serve on a lightly toasted bun with absolutely everything on it. Especially hot peppers.

Makes 3 large or 4 smaller burgers. *Perfect* ones.

## Burgers gone wild!

To the basic recipe you can add any of the following ingredients — but not all at once!

¼ cup (60 ml) bread crumbs
¼ cup (60 ml) finely chopped onion
1 clove garlic, minced or pressed
¼ cup (60 ml) barbecue sauce, ketchup or sriracha sauce
2 tbsp. (30 ml) grated Parmesan or cheddar cheese
1 tbsp. (15 ml) finely chopped parsley or green onion
1 tbsp. (15 ml) Worcestershire sauce

# Plain Old Meatballs

serves 4

*These are basic meatballs searching for fulfillment. Should they settle for spaghetti? Or should they wait for something more exotic and go Hawaiian? Or would they be wise to just go it alone on a toothpick? Only you can decide.*

1 lb. (500 g) lean ground beef (or turkey)
1 egg
½ cup (125 ml) bread crumbs
¼ cup (60 ml) finely chopped onion
1 tsp. (5 ml) salt
¼ tsp. (1 ml) black pepper

Preheat the oven to 375°F (190°C). Lightly grease a cookie sheet.

In a medium bowl, combine the ground beef, egg, bread crumbs, onion, salt and pepper. Smush together with a fork or clean bare hands until well mixed. Form into 1-inch (2 cm) balls, rolling them between your hands so they're nice and round. Place meatballs in one layer on the prepared cookie sheet and bake for 20 to 25 minutes, turning them over halfway through baking, or until lightly browned and cooked through.

Scoop the meatballs off the cookie sheet, leaving any fat that has drained out of them behind. Use in any recipe that calls for Plain Old Meatballs, such as Hawaiian Meatballs (see recipe on page 60), Killer Barbecue Meatballs (see recipe below) or Classic Spaghetti with Meatballs (see recipe on page 101).

# Killer Barbecue Meatballs serves 4

*Go ahead — be brave and add more cayenne pepper. Or don't. They're killer either way. And by killer, we mean delicious.*

1 batch Plain Old Meatballs (see recipe on page 58), browned
2 cups (500 ml) canned crushed tomatoes
1 cup (250 ml) ketchup
½ cup (125 ml) white or apple cider vinegar
½ cup (125 ml) brown sugar
½ medium onion, chopped
4 cloves garlic, minced or pressed
1 tbsp. (15 ml) Worcestershire sauce
1 tbsp. (15 ml) prepared mustard (Dijon, if you have it)
½ tsp. (2 ml) cayenne pepper (or more, if you like, or less, if you don't —
    they're your meatballs)

In a medium saucepan, combine the crushed tomatoes, ketchup, vinegar, brown sugar, onion, garlic, Worcestershire, mustard and cayenne. Place over medium heat and cook, stirring, for about 10 minutes. Taste, and adjust the seasoning to your spiciness comfort level. Plunk in the browned meatballs and continue to simmer, covered, for about 15 to 20 minutes, stirring occasionally.

Serve the meatballs over rice, with potatoes, or as an appetizer on toothpicks.

Makes about 4 servings as a main dish.

# Hawaiian Meatballs

*If it has pineapple in it, it must be from Hawaii, right? Well, maybe. Whatever —
it's good.*

1 batch Plain Old Meatballs (see recipe on page 58), browned
1 can (14 oz./398 ml) unsweetened pineapple chunks
¼ cup (60 ml) brown sugar
3 tbsp. (45 ml) white or apple cider vinegar
2 tbsp. (30 ml) cornstarch
2 tbsp. (30 ml) soy sauce
½ tsp. (2 ml) ground ginger (or 1 tbsp./15 ml grated fresh gingerroot)
1 green or red sweet pepper, cut into ½-inch (1 cm) squares
1 medium onion, cut into ½-inch (1 cm) squares
½ tsp. (2 ml) salt
¼ tsp. (1 ml) black pepper

Drain the pineapple chunks and pour the juice from the can into a measuring
cup. Add enough water to the juice to make a total of 1 1/4 cups (300 ml) of liquid. Pour this into a large saucepan or Dutch oven. (Restrain yourself from eating
all the pineapple chunks — you'll be needing them later.)

To the juice in the saucepan, add the brown sugar, vinegar, cornstarch, soy sauce
and ginger. Place over medium heat and bring the mixture to a simmer, stirring
constantly, until the sauce is clear and thickened. Dump in the entire batch of
browned meatballs, and simmer them in the sauce for 8 to 10 minutes, stirring
once or twice to prevent sticking. Add the green pepper, onion and pineapple
chunks, and continue to cook for 5 to 10 minutes, or until the vegetables are
tender but still crisp.

Serve immediately with hot cooked white or brown rice.

## Vegetarian alert!

Yes, vegetarians can have a perfectly acceptable shepherd's pie too! Just omit
the meat in the recipe opposite. Substitute 1½ cups (375 ml) TVP granules that
have been soaked in 1½ cups (375 ml) boiling vegetable broth for about 15
minutes. Otherwise, follow the recipe and voilà! Vegetarian Shepherd's Pie.

# Shepherd's Pie

*You don't have to be a shepherd to make this dish. Or to love it.*

2 tbsp. (30 ml) olive oil or vegetable oil
1 onion, chopped
2 cloves garlic, minced or pressed
1 medium sweet green or red pepper, chopped
2 cups (500 ml) sliced fresh mushrooms
1 medium carrot, peeled or scrubbed and diced
1½ lb. (750 g) lean ground beef, turkey or lamb
1 cup (250 ml) frozen peas
1 cup (250 ml) canned crushed tomatoes
1 tsp. (5 ml) salt, divided
½ tsp. (2 ml) black pepper, divided
4 large potatoes, peeled and cut into chunks
2 tbsp. (30 ml) butter
½ cup (125 ml) milk

Preheat the oven to 350°F (180°C).

Heat the oil in a large skillet over medium heat. Add the onion and garlic, and cook for about 5 minutes, or until softened. Add the peppers, mushrooms and carrots, and continue cooking for another 5 to 7 minutes, or until the carrots have started to soften. Add the ground beef, or whatever meat you're using, and cook, stirring to break up the clumps, for another 7 to 10 minutes, or until the meat is no longer pink. Add the peas, stir in the tomatoes, and season with about half of the salt and pepper. Continue to cook for 10 minutes, until the flavors are blended. Transfer to an 8- or 9-inch (20 or 23 cm) square baking dish.

While the meat mixture is cooking, prepare the mashed potato topping. Cook the potatoes in boiling water to cover, or steam them in a steamer basket over boiling water, until completely tender when poked with a fork. Drain thoroughly, then add milk and butter, and mash with a potato masher (or fork, if you don't have a masher) until fluffy. Season with the remaining salt and pepper. Spread the potato topping over the meat mixture in the baking dish, patting it down and swirling with a fork or spoon for a decorative touch. A sprinkle of paprika on top is a cheery touch if you happen to have some around. Place in the oven and bake for 35 to 40 minutes, or until the top is beginning to brown and the meat mixture is bubbling underneath.

# Totally Excellent Chili

*To be totally excellent, chili must be spicy (but not necessarily hot) and runny enough to eat with a spoon (but not soupy). Leave out or reduce the amount of hot pepper or cayenne if you prefer a mild chili — this dish will still have plenty of flavor.*

1½ lb. (750 g) lean ground beef
2 medium onions, chopped
2 cloves garlic, minced or pressed
1 can (28 oz./796 ml) diced tomatoes
1 tbsp. (15 ml) Mexican chili powder
2 tsp. (10 ml) ground cumin
1½ tsp. (7 ml) salt
½ tsp. (2 ml) curry powder
½ tsp. (2 ml) cayenne pepper (or one small fresh jalapeño pepper, minced —
    or both)
2 cans (19 oz./540 ml each) red kidney or pinto beans, drained and rinsed

In a large saucepan or Dutch oven, combine the ground beef with the onions and garlic, and cook, stirring to break up the clumps, until the meat is no longer pink and the onions are softened — about 10 minutes. Add the tomatoes, chili powder, cumin, salt, curry powder and cayenne or jalapeño, cover and simmer for about 30 minutes. Add the beans and cook for another 30 minutes, stirring often.

Serve this Totally Excellent Chili sprinkled with shredded cheese and accompanied by plain rice or freshly baked Corn Bread (see page 158). If the chili is too spicy for you, a spoonful of plain yogurt or sour cream will help cool things down.

# Mom's Dreaded Meat Loaf

serves 5–6

*Did your mom make this every Wednesday? Did you have to take meat loaf sandwiches to school? Did you hate them? Do you miss them now? Here — make this.*

1½ lb. (750 g) lean ground beef
1 cup (250 ml) soft bread crumbs
2 eggs, lightly beaten
1 medium onion, finely chopped
1 cup (250 ml) tomato juice
1 tsp. (5 ml) salt
½ tsp. (2 ml) black pepper
1 or 2 hard-boiled eggs, peeled
   (optional, but fun)
¼ cup (60 ml) ketchup

Preheat the oven to 350°F (180°C).

In a large bowl, combine the ground beef, bread crumbs, beaten eggs, onion, tomato juice, salt and pepper. Mix well, using your bare hands or a large fork, until everything is evenly combined. (Bare-handed mixing is a truly primal experience and highly recommended — but don't forget to wash your hands before and after.)

At this point you have two choices: You can either squish the mixture into a 9 x 5-inch (23 x 13 cm) loaf pan to bake (simple, straightforward, very fast), or you can shape a loaf by hand and bake it free-form in a 9 x 13-inch (23 x 33 cm) baking dish (this allows for more creative expression). Clearly you'll want to make your meat loaf exactly the way your mom did.

Wait! What about the hard-boiled eggs? So glad you asked. Bury them in the center of your meat loaf as a sort of hidden treasure. Looks cool when the meat loaf is sliced, but not critical to the success of the actual loaf.

With a basting brush, paint the surface of the meat loaf with the ketchup and bake for 1 hour and 15 minutes, or until cooked right through. Let stand 5 to 10 minutes before slicing.

Eat with mashed potatoes and something green.

# Steak Out!

Feeling carnivorous? Nothing satisfies a craving for pure, unadulterated meat like a good steak. Here are some pointers for buying and cooking that slab of beef.

## What kind?

If you're a steak-cooking novice, choose a boneless cut. Bones complicate the matter, so start with something simple.

For sheer beefy flavor and tenderness, and if you're willing to spend a little money, you can't go wrong with a strip loin or rib eye steak. It should be a minimum of 3/4 inch (1.5 cm) thick so that it can nicely brown on the surface without getting overcooked inside.

For a little less cash, look for top sirloin, sirloin tip or flank steak. You'll sacrifice a little tenderness, but these all have good flavor and should do the trick. A marinade will help.

If you buy your meat at a butcher shop, you can ask the butcher to recommend a cut of steak that will fit your budget and cooking technique. Some supermarkets that still do their own meat cutting will have a butcher in the back room who can help you pick the right steak for you. Don't be scared — most butchers are quite harmless once they put down that big sharp cleaver.

## What next?

Take the steak out of the refrigerator and let it come to room temperature for about 30 minutes or so before cooking. The meat will cook more evenly if it doesn't start out freezing cold.

For a rib eye or strip steak, just brush with olive oil and sprinkle with salt and pepper. No further glop needed.

For a sirloin or flank steak, place in a zip-top plastic bag and let it marinate (see ideas opposite) in the refrigerator for a couple of hours before cooking. Let it come to room temperature for 30 minutes before cooking, and sprinkle with salt and pepper just before cooking.

## Now to cook!

**On a barbecue grill:** Preheat the grill on high so it's nice and hot. Slap the meat on the grill and cook for about 3 minutes on each side (more if the steaks are extra thick, less if they're thin), turning over once. Cut a little slit into the middle of the meat to see if it's done to your liking — if not quite cooked enough, continue to grill in 1-minute increments until perfect. You do not want to overcook this thing.

**With an oven broiler:** Preheat the broiler for at least 5 minutes and arrange the oven rack so the meat is no more than 3 or 4 inches (7 to 10 cm) below the heat. Place the steak on a rack over a broiler pan and cook, about 3 to 5 minutes per side, turning once, or until done just the way you like it.

**Pan-seared:** You'll need a heavy skillet for this. This method will create a lot of smoke so you'll also need a good exhaust fan. Place the skillet — very lightly oiled — over medium-high heat for 4 or 5 minutes. The pan should be really, really hot. Slap the steak on the hot pan and cook 3 or 4 minutes per side, or until done the way you like it.

## To serve!

If it's one-person steaks, just put each steak on a plate and you're done.

If it's a large steak to share, slice crosswise into 1/2 to 1-inch strips. Arrange them on a plate and let people serve themselves.

And if it's a flank steak, you'll want to make sure you slice it crosswise, against the grain of the meat (you can see the grain lines running the length of the steak), into fairly thin slices. This steak has a lot of good flavor but can be chewy if not sliced the right way.

## Three marinade ideas

**Mediterranean Garlic and Herb:** Mix olive oil, minced or pressed garlic, chopped fresh rosemary (if you can find some), minced onion, salt, pepper and a little red wine if you have it. Don't worry about exact amounts — just mix everything until it smells good and add to the steaks.

**Soy and Garlic:** Soy sauce mixed with minced or pressed garlic, sesame oil and grated fresh ginger are all you need. Delicious.

**Chili Garlic:** Mix olive oil, minced or pressed garlic, minced fresh jalapeño pepper, minced onion and a little salt.

# Basic Beef Stew

*On a dark and stormy night, a good old bowl of beef stew is just the thing. Serve it with some decent bread and a salad and you'll feel very cozy.*

2 lb. (1 kg) beef stew meat, cut into 1-inch (2 cm) cubes (see note opposite)
½ tsp. (2 ml) salt
¼ tsp. (1 ml) black pepper
1 tbsp. (15 ml) olive oil or vegetable oil
1 medium onion, chopped
2 cloves garlic, minced or pressed
¼ cup (60 ml) beef broth or red wine
2½ cups (625 ml) tomato juice
2 medium carrots, cut into 1-inch (2 cm) chunks
1 tsp. (5 ml) dried thyme
2 medium potatoes, peeled and cubed

Preheat the oven to 375°F (190°C).

Toss the meat with the salt and pepper until evenly coated. Heat the oil in an oven-proof Dutch oven or casserole with a lid, and place over medium heat. Add the beef cubes — in batches, don't crowd them — and brown them slowly, turning the meat over so that all sides are evenly colored. When all the meat is done, remove the chunks from the pot and set aside.

Add the chopped onion and garlic to the pot, and sauté just until soft-ened — about 5 minutes. Add the broth or wine and stir to dissolve any crusty bits from the bottom of the pot. Now return the meat to the pot along with the tomato juice, carrots and thyme, and let the mixture come to a simmer. Cover the pot, place in the preheated oven and bake for 1 hour without peeking.

After 1 hour, remove the pot from the oven and add the potatoes, stirring to mix them into the liquid. Cover the pot and continue baking for at least 1 hour longer, until the meat is tender when you stick a fork into it. If it isn't quite tender enough, give it another 1/2 hour or so and test again.

## Stewing beef — what is it, anyway?

In the supermarket you'll sometimes find packages of something labeled stewing beef — all conveniently cut up and ready to cook. This is usually meat cut from a less tender part of the animal and it is perfect to use in stew. If stewing beef isn't available, choose a thick chuck steak — with or without bones – and cut it into chunks yourself. (Discard the bones or save them to add to Garbage Broth, see recipe on page 33.) Anything labeled shoulder, chuck, brisket, plate or blade will be good. If you're still confused, knock on the door of the supermarket meat department and ask. Butchers are usually more than happy to help you pick the right cut for what you're making.

# Omigod Pulled Pork serves 8–10

*Stupid easy, incredibly delicious. Buy a hunk of pork shoulder — sometimes called "butt" for no good reason — and feed a crowd for very little money. Brilliant.*

5 lb. (2.5 kg) pork shoulder butt, blade or picnic (so many names for basically the same thing) — bone in or boneless
1 tbsp. (15 ml) granulated sugar
1 tbsp. (15 ml) paprika
½ tbsp. (7 ml) salt
½ tbsp. (7 ml) cumin
½ tbsp. (7 ml) black pepper
½ tbsp. (7 ml) cayenne (or less — this is medium spicy)
1 tbsp. (15 ml) vegetable oil
2 cups (500 ml) water
½ to 1 cup (125 to 250 ml) barbecue sauce, any kind

Place the pork shoulder on a cutting board and, with a sharp knife, trim off any tough skin and excess fat and discard it. Don't try to remove every bit of the fat — it helps the meat remain moist as it cooks. And disregard the raggedy appearance of the trimmed meat — it won't matter in the end.

In a small bowl, stir together the sugar, paprika, salt, cumin, black pepper and cayenne. Sprinkle this mixture on all sides of the meat to coat it evenly. Place the pork on a plate and cover with plastic wrap. Refrigerate overnight. Letting the meat sit overnight allows the spice mixture to infuse the meat, but if you don't have the time, you can skip the overnight step and just proceed directly to cooking it. Preheat the oven to 325°F (160°C).

Remove the meat from the refrigerator and unwrap it. Heat the oil in a heavy Dutch oven or ovenproof casserole with a lid over medium-high heat. Brown the pork in the hot oil on all sides — 3 or 4 minutes per side — until well browned. Remove from heat. Add the water to the pot, cover with the lid and place in the preheated oven. Let cook, undisturbed, for 4 hours. Not kidding — this is a commitment. After 4 hours, lift the lid and poke a meat fork into the pork — it should go right through the meat without any resistance at all. Actually, the meat should really be just about falling apart. If it's not quite there, put it back in the oven for another 30 minutes to 1 hour.

When the pork is done, remove it from the oven and let cool for about 30 minutes, or until you can handle it. Remove it to a cutting board and, using two forks, shred the meat as much as possible into strands and place the strands in a bowl. You may have to chop the meat up a bit if the strands are too long. Discard the bone if there is one. There will be crusty bits on the surface and stringier bits in the middle — it's all good — just mix everything together.

Pour the liquid from the pot into a bowl or measuring cup. Remove as much of the fat from the surface as possible (you'll see the clear yellowish liquid floating at the top). Discard the fat and add the remaining liquid to the meat in the bowl. Stir in as much barbecue sauce as you think it needs and toss to mix.

Serve this crazy good pulled pork on soft buns with coleslaw (see recipe on page 44) and whatever else you like. Act humble when everyone goes nuts.

# Unfried Chicken

serves 3–4

*Better than takeout, crisp, delicious, easy — why would anyone not make this? Buy only your favorite chicken parts — breasts, drumsticks, whichever bits you like best — or start with a whole chicken and deconstruct it yourself (see instructions on page 80).*

1 cup (250 ml) dry bread crumbs
1 tbsp. (15 ml) grated Parmesan cheese
1 tsp. (5 ml) crumbled dried oregano or Italian seasoning
½ tsp. (2 ml) salt
¼ tsp. (1 ml) black pepper
2½ to 3 lb. (1 to 1.5 kg) chicken pieces (with skin and bones) or one medium
    chicken, cut into 8 pieces
2 to 3 tbsp. (30 to 45 ml) olive oil or
    vegetable oil

Preheat the oven to 375°F (190°C).

In a plastic or paper bag, combine the bread crumbs, Parmesan cheese, oregano or Italian seasoning, salt and pepper. Hold the top of the bag shut and shake to mix.

Place the chicken pieces in a bowl and drizzle with the oil. Mix well to

## Something's fishy with this chicken ...

Why, it's fish, of course! Instead of chicken, try this recipe with 1½ lb. (750 g) fish fillets — like tilapia, haddock or cod. Reduce the baking time to a total of 15 to 20 minutes, or until the fish flakes when you poke it with a fork.

lightly coat all the pieces. Drop 2 or 3 pieces of the oiled chicken at a time into the bag with the crumbs and shake until the chicken pieces are evenly coated with crumbs. Take them out of the bag and arrange the pieces on a rack placed over a baking sheet. (The rack allows the fat to drain from the chicken as it cooks.) Repeat with the remaining chicken pieces.

Place in the oven and bake for 45 to 50 minutes, turning all the pieces over halfway through, until the chicken is golden brown and crisp. To be sure the chicken is properly cooked right through, poke a fork into a thick section — if the juice that comes out is clear, not pink, the chicken is done.

### Fancy it up!

For something a little special, you can turn this plain unfried chicken into Chicken Parmigiana in a flash. Make the recipe as above, using only boneless, skinless chicken breasts. Arrange the cooked pieces in a baking dish, heat up some spaghetti sauce and spoon a little over each piece (store-bought sauce is fine). Sprinkle with shredded mozzarella cheese and grated Parmesan, and place in the oven (350°F/180°C) for about 10 minutes, or until the cheese is melted and the sauce is hot. Done.

# Baked Teriyaki Chicken serves 4

*Something magically delicious happens when homemade teriyaki sauce meets chicken pieces.*

½ cup (125 ml) soy sauce
½ cup (125 ml) granulated sugar
¼ cup (60 ml) cider vinegar or white vinegar
1 tbsp. (15 ml) cornstarch
2 cloves garlic, minced or pressed
1 tsp. (5 ml) ground ginger (or 1 tbsp./15 ml grated fresh gingerroot)
¼ tsp. (1 ml) black pepper
2 lb. (1 kg) skinless, boneless chicken thighs cut in half
1 tbsp. (15 ml) sesame seeds

Preheat the oven to 375°F (190°C). Grease a 9 x 13-inch (23 x 33 cm) rectangular baking dish or, for easier cleanup, line the baking dish with foil and grease the foil.

In a small saucepan, stir together the soy sauce, sugar, vinegar, cornstarch, garlic, ginger and pepper. Mix well to eliminate any lumps of cornstarch, then place over medium heat and cook, stirring constantly, until the sauce bubbles and becomes thick and glossy.

# The Ultimate Sloppy Joe serves 4

*Messy, runny, meaty, delicious. Go no further — you've arrived at Sloppy Joe perfection.*

2 tbsp. (30 ml) olive oil or vegetable oil
1 medium onion, chopped
1 stalk celery, chopped
1 cup (250 ml) coarsely chopped mushrooms
1 lb. (500 g) lean ground beef or turkey
¼ cup (60 ml) beef broth (prepared broth or made from bouillon cube or
    powder)
¼ cup (60 ml) ketchup
½ tsp. (2 ml) salt
½ tsp. (2 ml) sriracha or other hot pepper sauce (or more or less or none)
¼ tsp. (1 ml) black pepper

Heat the oil in a large skillet over medium heat. Add the onion, celery and mush-rooms, then cook, stirring occasionally, until soft — 7 to 10 minutes. Crumble in the ground beef or turkey and cook, stirring to break up the lumps, until the meat is no longer pink — 5 to 7 minutes. Add the broth, ketchup, salt and hot pepper sauce, and simmer for another 5 minutes, or until everything is nicely glopped together.

Spoon over 4 toasted hamburger buns and eat — sloppily.

# Fabulous Fajitas

*Fajitas are a great way to stretch a small amount of meat to serve a bunch of people. They're fun to assemble and even more fun to eat.*

1 lime, juice squeezed
2 tbsp. (30 ml) olive oil or vegetable oil (plus a bit more for cooking)
2 cloves garlic, minced or pressed
½ tsp. (2 ml) ground cumin
1 fresh jalapeño pepper, minced (optional)
¼ cup (60 ml) chopped cilantro
1 lb. (500 g) beef flank or sirloin steak *or* boneless, skinless chicken breasts
  (or some of each)
2 medium sweet red, green or yellow peppers, sliced into thick strips
1 large onion, sliced into thick strips
12 small (7-inch/18 cm) flour tortillas, warmed
Fajita toppings: Guacamole (see recipe on page 19), salsa, sour cream,
  shredded cheese, shredded lettuce, hot sauce, whatever you like!

In a small bowl, mix the lime juice, oil, garlic, cumin, jalapeño and cilantro. Place the steak or chicken breasts into a zip-top plastic bag and add the lime mixture. Press as much air out of the bag as possible and zip the top shut. Smoosh the bag around to coat the meat with the marinade and refrigerate for at least 1 hour (or overnight). If you're doing both steak and chicken, marinate them separately.

Place a large, heavy skillet over high heat. Drizzle in just enough oil to coat the pan, then remove the meat from the bag and place in the hot skillet. Cook steak for about 3 minutes per side, turning once, for medium-rare meat (longer if you prefer less rare). Chicken should be cooked until no longer pink inside — about 5 to 8 minutes per side. Remove to a plate and set aside while you cook the vegetables.

Add another drizzle of oil to the pan, reduce the heat slightly, toss in the onions and peppers, and cook, stirring constantly, for about 5 minutes, or until just soft-ened. Remove from heat.

Cut the steak, if you're using it, thinly across the grain (you'll see the grain run-ning lengthwise). Cut the chicken breasts into thin strips, any which way. Place sliced meat on a platter and surround with the onions and peppers.

Serve immediately with your choice of toppings (see above) and warmed flour tortillas. Let people roll their own perfect fajitas. *¡Qué bueno!*

## Veggie option

Instead of the steak or chicken, marinate sliced portobello mushrooms or sliced firm tofu, using the same marinade as used for meat. If you're serving both meat eaters and vegetarians, just double the marinade mixture and do both! Excellent.

You can grill the meat on the barbecue, if you have one available. (For details on grilling steak, see page 64.) The peppers and onions are still best stir-fried in a skillet, however.

# Rosemary Garlic Pork Tenderloin serves 2–3

*Pork tenderloin is the boneless chicken breast of pork. It's very lean, easy to cook and inexpensive when it goes on sale. One tenderloin usually weighs about 1 lb. (500 g) and serves 2 or 3 people. Double the recipe if you're feeding more than that.*

1 tbsp. (15 ml) olive oil or vegetable oil
1 tbsp. (15 ml) chopped fresh rosemary (or 1 tsp./5 ml dried)
2 cloves garlic, minced or pressed
1 tsp. (5 ml) salt
¼ tsp. (1 ml) black pepper
1 pork tenderloin (about 1 lb./500 g)
1 cup (250 ml) white wine or chicken broth (or some of each)

Preheat the oven to 400°F (200°C).

In a small bowl, mash together the oil, rosemary, garlic, salt and pepper. Smear this mixture all over the pork tenderloin. Tuck the two thin ends of the tenderloin under so that the meat is fairly even in thickness. Put a large (10-inch/25 cm) skillet on the stove over medium heat. Place the tenderloin in the pan and sear the meat, turning it over until it's browned on all sides — this should take about 10 minutes. (If your skillet isn't ovenproof, just transfer the meat to a baking dish after browning it.)

Pour the wine or broth into the skillet (or baking dish) and place it in the pre-heated oven. Bake for 10 minutes. Remove from the oven, cover the tenderloin with foil to keep warm and let it rest for 10 minutes (it's exhausted!). During this resting period, the meat will continue to cook, so don't skip this step.

Remove the meat to a cutting board, slice crosswise into 1/2-inch (1 cm) slices and serve with the sauce from the pan.

# Coconut Chicken Curry

*All the creamy deliciousness of chicken curry with none of the traditional ruckus that goes into making it. This curry is quite mild — if you want more heat, you can add another hot pepper or sprinkle in some cayenne when you add the curry powder.*

2 lb. (1 kg) skinless, boneless chicken breasts, cut into 1-inch (2 cm) chunks
1 tsp. (5 ml) salt
½ tsp. (2 ml) black pepper
1 tbsp. (15 ml) vegetable oil or coconut oil
2 tbsp. (30 ml) curry powder (hot or mild — your choice)
2 medium sweet peppers (any colour), cut into ½-inch (1 cm) squares
1 medium onion, chopped
2 cloves garlic, minced or pressed
1 fresh jalapeño (or other) hot pepper, seeded and sliced (optional)
1 can (14 oz./400 ml) coconut milk, regular or light
2 cups (500 ml) canned diced tomatoes (or diced fresh tomatoes)
1 tbsp. (15 ml) granulated sugar

In a bowl, toss the chicken chunks with the salt and pepper. Set aside.

In a large, deep skillet or Dutch oven, heat the oil over medium heat. Sprinkle in the curry powder and cook, stirring constantly, for about 1 minute, or until combined. Add the onion, garlic and jalapeño pepper (if you're using it), and continue to cook, stirring to coat with the spices, for 3 or 4 minutes, or until the onions are beginning to soften. Dump in the chicken chunks, raise the heat to medium high, and cook, stirring often, until the chicken has turned mostly opaque.

Add the coconut milk, tomatoes and sugar to the pan, and bring to a boil. Lower the heat to medium, and simmer, uncovered, stirring occasionally, for 15 to 20 minutes. Serve with plain basmati or jasmine rice.

## Bones or boneless? Skin or skinless?

Lots to choose from in the chicken section of the supermarket. If chicken bones and skin gross you out, buy boneless and skinless pieces. If, on the other hand, you like a little something to gnaw on and skin doesn't bother you, go with bone-in, skin-on chicken (it's usually the cheaper option). Most recipes will work either way, but cooking time may be slightly shorter for boneless pieces.

# Good Old Roast Chicken

serves 3–4

*Almost everyone likes a roast chicken dinner. It's familiar, delicious and very homey. Plus, it makes for great leftovers the next day — if there are any leftovers, that is.*

1 medium to large chicken (3 to 4 lb./1.5 to 2 kg)
2 cloves garlic, minced or pressed
1 tbsp. (15 ml) olive oil or vegetable oil
1 tsp. (5 ml) salt
1 tsp. (5 ml) paprika
½ tsp. (2 ml) black pepper

Preheat the oven to 375°F (190°C).

Place the chicken on a plate and pat it dry with paper towel. In a small bowl, mash together the garlic, oil, salt, paprika and pepper, stirring to make a thick paste.

By hand or with a basting brush (if you have such a thing), rub the garlic paste all over the chicken, inside and outside. (Pretend you're applying sunscreen at the beach.)

Put the chicken into a roasting pan — a rectangular baking pan or even a foil pan will do — and roast, uncovered, for 1 1/2 to 2 hours, basting with the pan juices occasionally, until the chicken is a deep golden brown and a leg moves easily when you wiggle it. When you stab the chicken with a fork, the juices that run out should be clear, not pink. If you're still not sure whether the chicken is done, poke an instant-read meat thermometer into a thick part of the thigh (not touching the bone). It should read 165°F (74°C) when the chicken is done.

Remove from the oven and let rest for about 5 minutes before cutting it up. Resting time makes the chicken easier to handle and it won't leak as much juice.

Serves, oh, maybe 3 or 4, depending on who you're feeding and exactly how big the chicken is.

# Chicken Cacciatore

serves 4

*This saucy Italian classic is guaranteed to warm up the chilliest winter evening. Spoon it over some pasta, add a crusty loaf of bread and a nice salad — perfetto.*

3 lb. (1.5 kg) chicken pieces — bone-in thighs or
    breasts or one whole medium chicken, cut up
2 tbsp. (30 ml) all-purpose flour
½ tsp. (2 ml) salt
¼ tsp. (1 ml) black pepper
1 tbsp. (15 ml) olive oil or vegetable oil
1 medium onion, chopped
1 sweet green pepper, chopped
8 oz. (250 g) fresh mushrooms, thickly sliced
    (about 2 cups/500 ml sliced)
2 cloves garlic, minced or pressed
1 tsp. (5 ml) crumbled dried oregano
½ tsp. (2 ml) crumbled dried thyme
1 can (28 oz./796 ml) diced tomatoes
½ cup (125 ml) chicken broth (prepared broth
    or made from bouillon cube or powder)
¼ cup (60 ml) tomato paste (about half of a 5.5
    oz./156 ml can)
⅓ cup (75 ml) chopped fresh parsley

Trim all the excess fat and hangy bits from the chicken pieces, and discard them. Place the chicken in a large bowl, sprinkle with the flour, salt and pepper, and toss to coat evenly.

In a Dutch oven or large saucepan with a lid, heat the oil over medium-high heat. Working with just 3 or 4 pieces at a time, brown the chicken in the hot oil, turning over to brown all sides well. Remove chicken pieces to a plate once they're browned and continue until all the pieces are done.

Pour out all except for about 1 tbsp. (15 ml) of the fat from the pot. Add the onion, pepper, mushrooms, garlic, oregano and thyme, and cook, stirring occasionally, until the vegetables are softened — about 6 to 8 minutes. Add the tomatoes, broth and tomato paste, and bring the mixture to a boil. Add the browned chicken pieces to the sauce, then turn the heat down to low and cook, covered, for 20 to 25 minutes, stirring occasionally. Taste, and adjust seasoning with salt and pepper if needed. Sprinkle with chopped parsley and serve immediately.

## How to cut up a chicken

Oh yuck. You've got yourself a whole chicken and now you have to dismantle it. Although you don't need a degree in veterinary medicine to take a chicken apart, getting to know your victim before you begin is helpful.

Lay the bird out on the counter, belly up, and examine it for a couple of minutes. Move the various appendages so you can feel where the joints are and how everything hooks together. Flap the wings, walk the chicken around on its drumsticks and have it do a little chicken dance around the table. Sound effects are useful to help you get into the mood. Okay, that's enough. Now get to work.

Using a sharp knife or, better yet, a pair of good sharp kitchen shears, cut the chicken lengthwise through the breast from the tail end to the neck end. Now open the chicken up like a book and cut alongside the backbone from one end to the other. You will now have two more or less identical halves. Feel for the joint where the drumstick attaches to the body and then cut the drumstick off. There is a place where it detaches fairly easily, so keep poking around with your knife until you find the right spot. Next, remove the whole wing in a similar fashion. Finally, separate the breast section from the thigh by cutting the two sections apart along the curve of the thigh. Then, with a final whack, hack through the backbone to separate the two parts. There. Now do the same thing to the other half.

If you have followed these instructions, you will end up with 2 drumsticks, 2 wings, 2 breasts and 2 thighs. (If you have gone berserk, you may have more pieces.) You can now either cook the entire bird, or cook some of it immediately and wrap the remaining pieces individually in plastic or foil and freeze them for a rainy day. Don't forget to label the packages!

# Honey Garlic Wings

serves 3–4

*If you eat these wings with your hands, sitting in front of the TV, they're a snack. On a plate, at the table, they're a meal. Either way, these wings are delicious.*

3 lb. (1.5 kg) chicken wings (about 18 wings)
4 cloves garlic, peeled
1 cup (250 ml) honey or brown sugar
½ cup (125 ml) water
¼ cup (60 ml) soy sauce
1 tbsp. (15 ml) white vinegar or apple cider vinegar
1 tsp. (5 ml) ground ginger (or 1 tbsp./15 ml grated fresh gingerroot)

Preheat the oven to 375°F (190°C).

Trim the pointy tips off each wing and discard them, or save to use when making Chicken Soup (see recipe on page 32) or Garbage Broth (see recipe on page 33). Cut each wing in half at the elbow. Arrange wings in a single layer in a baking dish just large enough to hold them all.

In a food processor or blender, combine the garlic cloves, honey or brown sugar, water, soy sauce, vinegar and ginger. Whirl until smooth. Pour this mixture over the wings and stir around to coat. Bake for 15 minutes, turn the wings over in the sauce and continue to bake for another 15 to 20 minutes, or until the wings are browned and the sauce is nice and sticky.

Eat them just like that — straight from the pan. Or be a grown-up about it and serve them on a plate with some rice to sop up the extra sauce.

Makes 3 to 4 servings. Or less.

# Thermonuclear Buffalo Wings   serves 1–4

*These wings are an easy version of the Buffalo classic, which is traditionally served with celery sticks and blue cheese dressing (a pairing that has always seemed a bit strange). Go ahead and add extra hot pepper sauce, if you want, or reduce the amount to avoid Total Meltdown. Your choice.*

2 lb. (1 kg) chicken wings (about 12 wings)
½ cup (125 ml) all-purpose flour
1 tsp. (5 ml) salt
½ tsp. (2 ml) black pepper
¼ cup (60 ml) hot pepper sauce (*less* for the timid, *more* for the brave)
2 tbsp. (30 ml) butter
1 tbsp. (15 ml) white vinegar or cider vinegar

Preheat the oven to 375°F (190°C).

Trim the pointy tips off each wing and discard them, or save to add when making Chicken Soup (see recipe on page 32) or Garbage Broth (see recipe on page 33). Cut each wing in half at the elbow. Put the flour, salt and pepper into a small bag and shake to combine. Toss in 3 or 4 pieces of wing at a time, hold the top closed and shake until wings are evenly coated. Remove the floured wings to a baking pan or cookie sheet, and repeat until all the wings are done. Place in the oven and bake for 15 minutes. Turn the wings over and bake for another 15 or 20 minutes, or until crisp and browned.

While the wings are baking, combine the hot pepper sauce, butter and vinegar in a small saucepan. Stir until the butter is melted and sauce is hot, then remove from heat. As soon as the wings are done, remove them to a bowl, drizzle with the hot sauce mixture and toss to coat evenly.

Serve immediately. With or without celery sticks and blue cheese dressing.

Makes 16 to 20 wings — between 1 and 4 servings, depending.

# Fried Rice with Whatever          serves 3–4

*Fried rice — a brilliant invention — is best when made with cold leftover rice and whatever bits of stuff you happen to have in your fridge. Vegetarians can just skip the meat and double the vegetables or use firm tofu in place of the meat.*

2 tbsp. (30 ml) vegetable oil
1 medium onion, chopped
2 cloves garlic, minced or pressed
1 egg, beaten
2 cups (500 ml) diced or sliced fresh, frozen or cooked vegetables (any mixture of whatever you have around — celery, green pepper, mushrooms, carrots, bean sprouts, green beans, broccoli, zucchini, peas, baby spinach leaves)
2 cups (500 ml) diced cooked meat or fish of any kind (chicken, beef, pork, shrimp, turkey, groundhog and so on)
3 cups (750 ml) leftover cooked rice
2 tbsp. (30 ml) soy sauce
1 tsp. (5 ml) sesame oil (if you have it — it's very nice)
4 green onions, sliced

In a wok or large skillet, heat the vegetable oil over high heat. Add the onion and garlic, and stir-fry for 1 or 2 minutes, until the onion is slightly softened. Stir in the egg and cook the mixture just until the egg is scrambled — this won't even take a minute. Toss in the vegetables — whatever you're using — the ones that take the longest time to cook first, then the next and the next and the next, adding any cooked vegetables only at the last minute. Generally, soft watery vegetables (like zucchini and bean sprouts) will cook faster than hard ones (like carrots and celery). But really, don't go all technical about this. It isn't rocket science — it's just dinner.

When the vegetables are all in the wok or skillet, throw in the meat and stir everything a bit. Since this ingredient is already cooked, you just need to heat it. Now add the rice and keep stirring. Add the soy sauce and cook the whole business, stirring and tossing, for 2 or 3 minutes, until everything is hot and well mixed. Sprinkle in the sesame oil if you're using it and the green onions. Toss it all around, remove from heat and serve immediately.

## Dribs-and-Drabs Stir-Fry

This is not a recipe. Well, not exactly. Only you know what dribs and drabs lurk in the darkest recesses of your refrigerator. Half a withered onion. Two pitiful carrots. A pathetic, lonesome, partially eaten chicken leg. Seven green beans (why did you keep seven green beans?). This sorry collection is about to turn into dinner. Really.

Start by cutting up everything you can find into smallish pieces — arrange these attractively on a large platter (or a couple of plates). Put all the cooked stuff (leftover pot roast, yesterday's broccoli, half a can of corn) together on one plate since these won't require as much stir-frying as the raw stuff (hunk of green pepper, slab of cabbage, sliver of bacon). The stir-fry is already starting to feel like something, isn't it?

Now make up a sauce. In a small bowl, stir together 2 tsp. (10 ml) cornstarch, 2 tbsp. (30 ml) soy sauce and ½ cup (125 ml) water, broth or vegetable juice (like the liquid from a can of peas or something).

Okay. Start frying. Heat 2 tbsp. (30 ml) of vegetable oil in a wok or large skillet over high heat. Definitely throw in some chopped or sliced onion to start. This always smells productive. Now add the raw stuff — meat first, if you've got some, then the hard vegetables (like carrots), then the softer things (like mushrooms). Stir-fry, tossing constantly, until the meat is cooked and the vegetables are looking hopeful. Now add the cooked bits, a little at a time, until everything is in, and stir-fry for a couple of minutes more.

Stir the sauce mixture (the cornstarch will have settled to the bottom of the bowl) and add it all at once to the skillet. Cook, stirring constantly, for about a minute, until slightly thickened and bubbly. Remove from the heat and serve over hot cooked rice or pasta.

Wow. And you thought there was nothing in the house to eat.

# The leftover zone

Leftovers are your friends. They are always there for you, waiting patiently in the fridge, ready for you to eat at any moment. Why do we treat them so badly? Here are some ways to show those loyal leftovers how much we really appreciate them.

**Heat them up and serve just the way you did the first time around.**
In most cases, a microwave does this best — retaining most of the taste and texture of the original.

**Don't bother to heat them up.**
Discover how the flavor of a hot food changes when it's cold. Cold leftover pizza actually makes a good, quick breakfast.

**Make a sandwich out of them.**
Meat loaf, chicken, meatballs, pot roast — they all make an excellent sandwich if you slice them thin enough and add some lettuce, tomato, onion, pickle, mayonnaise, mustard, whatever. Allegedly, leftover spaghetti makes a great sandwich, but this has not yet been confirmed scientifically.

**Give them another life altogether.**
Reincarnate those potatoes as a potato salad. Turn those leftover vegetables into soup. Give those shreds of chicken or turkey new life as a stir-fry. Create a brand-new dinner from old food — you can make a silk purse out of a sow's ear. Or at the very least, a casserole.

**Create a do-it-yourself TV dinner.**
Recycle that multicompartment plate (the kind you get with a frozen dinner) by filling it with the leftovers of a previously enjoyed meal. Mashed potatoes here, a slice or two of meat loaf there, a few pieces of broccoli in the corner. Cover with foil and freeze for another day. (Hint: Don't freeze the salad. You've been warned.)

# Something Fishy

# Fish à la Foil

*The ultimate convenience food. This cooks in minutes, and if you eat it right out of the foil, there are no dishes to wash. Use any type of fish fillet you like, but try to make a responsible choice when you shop.*

2 tbsp. (30 ml) butter, melted
2 tbsp. (30 ml) chopped fresh parsley
1 tbsp. (15 ml) lemon juice
1½ lb. (750 g) fish fillets, defrosted if frozen
1 tsp. (5 ml) salt
¼ tsp. (1 ml) black pepper
2 medium carrots, coarsely grated
1 medium onion, chopped
1 cup (250 ml) shredded Swiss or cheddar cheese

Preheat the oven to 425°F (230°C). Have ready four 12-inch (30 cm) squares of heavy-duty aluminum foil and grease them lightly.

In a small bowl, combine the butter, parsley and lemon juice. In another bowl, combine the carrots, onion and cheese.

On each square of foil, spread some of the parsley mixture, dividing it evenly among the 4 portions. Top each with 1 serving of fish (again, divide the fish evenly among the 4 squares) and sprinkle with salt and pepper. Top the fish with the vegetable-and-cheese mixture. Fold the foil into packets, forming a tight seal on top and at the sides.

Place the packets on a baking sheet and bake in the preheated oven for 15 to 20 minutes.

Remove the packets from the oven, place 1 packet on each plate and allow each eater to peel open their own. Surprise!

## Frozen or fresh?

Although you would think that fresh fish is, well, fresher, this may not be the case. Fish that has been flash-frozen at the source is often fresher than fish that's been shipped across the country (or across the world). Properly cooked, you probably couldn't tell the difference.

# Crispy Potato Chip Fish

serves 4

*Absolutely juvenile! Totally unsophisticated! Very crunchy and delicious.*

½ cup (125 ml) Creamy Italian Dressing (see recipe on page 49 or use store-
  bought dressing)
1½ lb. (750 g) fish fillets
3 cups (750 ml) potato chips, plain or flavored
½ cup (125 ml) shredded cheddar cheese

Preheat the oven to 400°F (200°C). Grease a rimmed cookie sheet.

Pour the salad dressing into a shallow bowl. Dip each fillet into the dressing,
turning to coat both sides. Arrange in a single layer on the greased cookie sheet.

Put the potato chips in a large, heavy-duty, zip-top plastic bag and zip it shut,
leaving a tiny opening for the air to escape. Now, using a rolling pin or wine
bottle, crush the potato chips to smithereens. Sprinkle the crushed chips evenly
over the fish on the cookie sheet. Top with the shredded cheese. Place in the
preheated oven and bake for about 20 minutes, or until the fish flakes when you
poke it with a fork.

# Maple Glazed Salmon

serves 4

*Seriously — what part of that doesn't sound amazing? Marinate the fish while
you make a salad or cook some potatoes.*

⅓ cup (75 ml) maple syrup
⅓ cup (75 ml) soy sauce
2 tbsp. (30 ml) cider vinegar
2 cloves garlic, minced or pressed
1½ lb. (750 g) salmon fillet, cut into serving-size pieces

Preheat the oven to 400°F (200°C). Grease a baking dish large enough to hold
the salmon pieces in a single layer.

Measure the maple syrup, soy sauce, vinegar and garlic into a small jar (an empty jam jar or whatever you have handy). Shake to combine ingredients. Place the
salmon fillets in a shallow dish or zip-top plastic bag. Add the maple marinade
and cover the dish with plastic wrap, or zip the bag shut and press the air out.
Refrigerate for at least 30 minutes (but not longer than 1 hour).

Remove the salmon from the marinade and place in the prepared baking dish (discard the marinade — it has done its job). Bake, uncovered, for about 20 minutes, or until the fish flakes easily when you poke it with a fork.

# Greek Baked Shrimp with Feta     serves 4

*You can serve this fantastic dish as a main course or as an appetizer. It's almost too good to be so easy.*

2 tbsp. (30 ml) olive oil or vegetable oil
1 medium onion, chopped
2 cloves garlic, minced or pressed
1 cup (250 ml) chopped green onions (one bunch)
2 cups (500 ml) diced tomatoes (canned or fresh)
½ cup (125 ml) white wine, broth or water
¼ cup (60 ml) chopped fresh parsley
1 tsp. (5 ml) dried oregano
1 tsp. (5 ml) salt
¼ tsp. (1 ml) black pepper
2 lb. (1 kg) raw shrimp, medium or large, shelled
½ cup (125 ml) crumbled feta cheese

Preheat the oven to 450°F (230°C). Grease a 9 or 10-inch (23 or 25 cm) round or square baking dish.

Heat the oil in a medium skillet over medium heat. Add the onion and cook, stirring, until just starting to soften — about 3 minutes. Add the garlic and green onions, and cook, stirring, for 2 minutes, then add the tomatoes, wine or broth or water (whichever you're using), parsley, oregano, salt and pepper. Bring to a boil, then reduce the heat to low and simmer, uncovered, for about 15 minutes, or until thickened. (You can spend this time shelling shrimp or making a salad. Just a thought.)

Spoon about half the tomato sauce into the prepared baking dish and top with the shrimp, spreading them out evenly. Dollop the remaining tomato sauce over the shrimp and sprinkle evenly with the crumbled feta cheese. Put the baking dish in the oven and bake for 15 to 20 minutes, or until the sauce is bubbling, the shrimp in the center of the dish are pink and the feta cheese is lightly browned.

Serve hot with crusty bread to mop up the delicious sauce.

Makes about 4 servings as a main dish, 6 to 8 servings as an appetizer.

## Shrimp factoids

**Shells on or shells off?** Raw shrimp are sold both with and without their shells. Generally, shell-on shrimp will be less expensive per pound than shelled ones. Since most recipes ask you to remove the shells before cooking, which kind is a better choice — shell on or shell off? Peeling shrimp is not really that much work, so if price is an issue and you're willing to spend a little time, buy shrimp in the shell and peel them yourself. But if you really don't want to be bothered doing all that shell removal, go ahead and buy shelled shrimp.

**What about the veins?** Often a recipe will tell you to devein shrimp before cooking. Why? Well, it's mostly appearance (the black vein looks unsightly), but a large black vein may also have grit and other weird stuff in it. So if the vein is small and you don't mind the look, don't worry about it. But if the vein creeps you out, remove it with a sharp knife before cooking. Not a lot of extra work.

# Chowder from the Black Lagoon serves 4

*If you're using frozen fish, don't bother thawing it before cooking. Just hack it into chunks and plunk them in the pot. With a salad and some good bread, you've got dinner in less than half an hour.*

2 tbsp. (30 ml) butter
1 medium onion, chopped
3 medium potatoes, peeled and cut into ½-inch (1 cm) cubes
2 medium carrots, diced
2 cups (500 ml) milk
1 tsp. (5 ml) salt
½ tsp. (2 ml) dried thyme
1 lb. (500 g) fish fillets (like tilapia, haddock, cod or other white fish)
2 cups (500 ml) thickly sliced fresh mushrooms
2 tbsp. (30 ml) chopped fresh parsley

Melt the butter in a large saucepan or Dutch oven over medium heat. Add the onion and cook until just softened, about 5 minutes. Stir in the potatoes, carrots, milk, salt and thyme. Bring to a boil, then reduce the heat to medium low and let simmer for about 15 minutes, or until the potatoes are nearly tender.

Cut the fish fillets into 1 1/2-inch (4 cm) chunks and add to the pot along with the mushrooms and the parsley. Stir to mix well, bring back to a boil over medium heat, then reduce the heat to medium low and simmer for about 10 minutes, or until the fish is cooked (it will be opaque and break into flakes easily when poked with a fork). This makes quite a thick chowder. If you prefer it to be soupier, just add a bit more milk to thin it.

# Shrimp in Garlic Butter

*Shrimp. Garlic. Butter. Sure — go ahead and do it. You know you want to. Serve these shrimp tossed with pasta, spooned over rice or just with some crusty bread to soak up the garlic butter.*

¼ cup (60 ml) butter, melted
2 tbsp. (30 ml) olive oil
4 cloves garlic, minced or pressed
¼ cup (60 ml) chopped green onions
½ tsp. (2 ml) paprika
½ tsp. (2 ml) hot pepper flakes (optional, but good)
½ tsp. (2 ml) salt
¼ tsp. (1 ml) black pepper
2 lb. (1 kg) raw shrimp, as large as you can afford, shelled
2 tbsp. (30 ml) chopped fresh parsley

Preheat the broiler element of your oven to high. Place the top oven rack as close to the broiler element as possible.

In a large bowl, stir together the butter, oil, garlic, green onions, paprika, hot pepper flakes, salt and pepper. Add the shrimp and toss to coat them evenly with the butter mixture. Spread the shrimp out in a single layer on a rimmed cookie sheet or shallow baking dish.

Put the pan on the top oven rack and broil for 2 to 3 minutes, until the shrimp begin to turn pink; then stir, flip the shrimp over and return them to the oven to broil for another 2 to 3 minutes. The shrimp should be pink and slightly curled — but don't overcook them or they'll get rubbery. Sprinkle with parsley and serve immediately with bread, pasta or rice.

Makes 4 servings. Less, if you're pigs about it.

# Mussels in White Wine

*Insanely easy, ridiculously cheap and amazingly delicious. Look the mussels over very carefully before cooking and discard any that don't close up when you tap on the shell. (Hello? Hello? Anyone home?) Give them a little scrub and a rinse, and they're ready to cook.*

2 tbsp. (30 ml) olive oil or butter
½ medium onion, finely chopped
4 cloves garlic, minced or pressed
½ tsp. (2 ml) hot pepper flakes (or to taste)
½ tsp. (2 ml) salt
1½ cups (375 ml) white wine
2 lb. (1 kg) mussels, scrubbed and rinsed
½ cup (125 ml) chopped fresh parsley

In a large pot, heat the oil or butter over medium heat. Add the onion and garlic, and cook, stirring, just until the onion softens. Add the hot pepper flakes and salt, stir for a few seconds, then pour in the wine. Bring to a boil and let simmer for a minute or two.

Toss in the mussels, stir to mix, then cover the pan and let boil for about 2 minutes. The shells will start to open as the mussels cook. Add the parsley, stir again and let cook for just 1 or 2 minutes longer, until all the shells are open. (Discard any mussels that refuse to open after cooking — nobody wants to eat a mussel with a bad attitude.)

Serve immediately with good bread to sop up the delicious sauce.

Makes 2 servings as a main dish or 4 servings as an appetizer.

# Tuna or Salmon Burgers

*These burgers are delicious and easy to make, and will satisfy that primal need for something charred on a bun. Serve with all the usual burger toppings.*

1 can (6.5 oz./184 g) tuna or salmon, drained
1½ cups (375 ml) fresh bread crumbs
½ medium onion, finely chopped
1 medium carrot, coarsely grated
1 egg
2 tbsp. (30 ml) mayonnaise
1 tsp. (5 ml) vegetable oil
½ tsp. (2 ml) salt
¼ tsp. (1 ml) black pepper
Toasted buns, toppings — the works

In a medium bowl, mix all the ingredients (except the buns and toppings, of course) together until well mushed. If you have a food processor, now is the time to use it. The tuna or salmon mixture must be finely chopped or the burgers won't hold together on the grill. If you don't have a processor, use a fork and mash like crazy. By hand, form the mixture into compact patties.

Brush both sides of the burgers lightly with vegetable oil. Place on a preheated barbecue grill and cook over medium-high heat for 5 or 6 minutes per side, or until golden brown. Serve in a bun with sliced tomato, mayonnaise and lettuce. Oh, and okay, ketchup or sriracha sauce, and maybe some onion too.

You can also pan-fry these burgers if you don't have a barbecue grill. Heat a small amount of vegetable oil in a large skillet and cook the patties on both sides until golden. You can serve very tiny patties as tuna or salmon nuggets with dipping sauce.

# Primarily Pasta

# Pasta Basics

Just exactly how much pasta is too much? Or worse, how much is too little? And how do you cook the stuff?

## For one serving
- Long pasta (spaghetti, fettuccine or linguine): 3/4-inch (2 cm) diameter bunch
- Medium-size macaroni shapes (elbows, small shells, fusilli): 1 cup (250 ml)
- Large-size macaroni shapes (rotini, rigatoni, large penne): 1 1/2 cups (375 ml)
- Egg noodles (or other cut noodles): 1 2/3 cups (400 ml)

## Unscientific shortcut
Macaroni will approximately double in volume when cooked. So if you think you can eat a whole bowlful of macaroni, fill the bowl halfway with the dry pasta and that should end up being about right.

## Another unscientific hint
A 2-lb. (900 g) package of pasta will serve about 8 people as a main dish. Use half a package for 4 servings.

## Cooking the stuff
Fill your largest pot with water, add a spoonful of salt and bring to a full boil over high heat. If you cover the pot, the water will boil faster. Uncover, and add the pasta to the boiling water — the water will stop boiling temporarily because the pasta lowers the water temperature. Stir until the water returns to a boil to prevent the pasta sticking to the bottom of the pot, then cook until done, stirring occasionally. Don't cover the pot while the pasta is cooking — that can cause a messy boil-over.

## How can you tell when it's done?
Small, thin pasta will cook more quickly than big, fat pasta. Start tasting after 5 minutes. The pasta should be tender but still a little chewy through the middle (in Italian this is called *al dente*, meaning "to the tooth"). If you're cooking spaghetti, you can use the ever-popular Wall Test: Throw a strand against the wall, and if it sticks, it's done. (This test is not recommended, however, for rough stucco walls or brick walls or when neat-freak friends or relatives are watching.)

## Chopping tomatoes
The fastest way to chop up a lot of ripe tomatoes is to put them in a big bowl and mush them up with your bare hands. Just dive in there and squish away to your heart's content. Totally gross, very effective, really fun.

Drain the pasta thoroughly in a strainer or colander and dump it immediately into a serving bowl or back into the cooking pot to toss with your sauce. Do not rinse the cooked pasta unless you want to cool it quickly to use in another recipe — like pasta salad or a macaroni casserole.

## Pasta trivia

Adding a spoonful of oil to the cooking water does absolutely nothing useful, no matter what anyone tells you. It does not prevent the pasta from sticking together and it doesn't prevent the pot from boiling over. Better just keep an eye on the stove and be careful not to overcook.

Salt doesn't help the water boil faster. It does, however, make the water salty and enhance the flavor of the cooked pasta. Or you can just add salt when you're saucing the pasta. Either way works.

If your pot starts to boil over, just blow hard over the surface and it should settle down. Meanwhile, lower the heat slightly to keep that from happening again.

Don't get stuck in a pasta rut. Elbows and spaghetti aren't the only things out there, you know. Have you ever tried fusilli? Or radiatore? Or farfalle? Each shape tastes different. Go ahead — see for yourself.

### Pantry raid!

Dead of winter, no fresh tomatoes — what to do? Instead of the fresh plum tomatoes in the recipe opposite, substitute 3 cans (28 oz./796 ml each) whole or diced tomatoes to make this very same sauce. Since they're already peeled, you can skip that step. Easy and delicious.

### To peel or not to peel? Decisions, decisions.

It's true — tomato skin has an annoying tendency to curl itself into pointy little bits in your otherwise perfect pasta sauce. But it's also true that peeling tomatoes is a pain. Only you can decide whether getting rid of the skin is worth the effort.

If you decide to peel, here's one way to make that pesky job easier.

Boil a pot of water. Have a bowl of cold water nearby. Working with one tomato at a time, stab it on a fork and submerge it in the boiling water for no more than 10 seconds. Dunk the tomato in the cold water until just cool enough to handle. Gently pull the skin off — it should practically peel itself. Done.

# Big Batch Spaghetti Sauce

*Every summer millions of innocent tomatoes wither and rot simply because they have no one to love them and use them. This senseless waste must stop! Go seek out a big basket of perfectly ripe tomatoes, bring it home and make a vat of spaghetti sauce. (If you can find plum tomatoes, they are great for making sauce — they're more solid so it takes less time to cook to the right thickness.)*

¼ cup (60 ml) olive oil or vegetable oil

2 medium onions, chopped

4 to 6 cloves garlic, minced or pressed

5 lb. (2.5 kg) ripe tomatoes, peeled (or not — see page 98) and chopped (18 to 20 medium tomatoes)

2 tbsp. (30 ml) tomato paste

1 tsp. (5 ml) salt

½ tsp. (2 ml) black pepper

½ cup (125 ml) chopped fresh herbs — parsley, basil, oregano, whatever (or 2 tsp./10 ml each dried basil and oregano)

## Spaghetti sauce gone wild!

This recipe makes a very basic tomato sauce, devoid of extraneous bits like mushrooms or peppers. But you go right ahead and put your personal stamp on this by adding whatever you like to the sauce. Raw vegetables or meat should be added at the beginning, with the onions. Additional herbs or spices can go in with the tomatoes.

In your largest pot, heat the oil and sauté the onions and garlic over medium heat for 5 to 7 minutes, or until softened. Dump in the chopped tomatoes and bring to a boil, stirring often. Add the tomato paste, salt, pepper and dried herbs (if you're using them). Reduce the heat to medium low and let the whole business simmer (no lid) for 45 minutes to 1 hour, stirring frequently to prevent the sauce from scorching and sticking to the bottom of the pot. It should gradually thicken as the tomatoes break down and the water evaporates.

When the sauce is nearly thick enough, add any fresh herbs and simmer for another 15 minutes or so. Your homemade sauce may not be as thick as store-bought spaghetti sauce because you're not using any starches or thickeners — this is a good thing, so don't worry about it. If you really think your sauce is too thin, add another spoonful or two of tomato paste and cook until blended and thickened. If you prefer a smooth-textured sauce, you can use an immersion blender to get rid of the lumps.

Use this sauce immediately over pasta or in lasagna, or pack into plastic bags or containers and freeze.

Makes about 6 cups (1.5 liters).

# Fettuccine with Asparagus and Cream

serves 4

*This is where asparagus wants to go when it dies. Asparagus nirvana. Save this killer recipe for a special occasion.*

½ cup (125 ml) whipping cream
¼ cup (60 ml) butter, softened to room temperature
1 cup (250 ml) grated Parmesan cheese
1 lb. (500 g) fresh asparagus, trimmed and cut in 1-inch (2 cm) pieces
1 tbsp. (15 ml) olive oil
2 green onions, sliced
1 lb. (500 g) uncooked fettuccine
½ tsp. (2 ml) salt
¼ tsp. (1 ml) black pepper

In a bowl, with an electric mixer, beat together the whipping cream and the butter until creamy. Add the Parmesan cheese and beat until smooth. Set aside.

Place the asparagus pieces in a steamer basket over boiling water and steam for 3 to 5 minutes, just until the asparagus turns bright green. Dump the asparagus immediately into a bowl of cold water to stop it from cooking any further. Drain well and set aside.

Heat the olive oil in a large skillet over medium heat. Add the green onions and stir for 2 minutes, then toss in the asparagus and let cook for just a minute more, until heated through. Remove from heat.

Cook the fettuccine in a large pot of boiling water until tender but not mushy. Drain, then dump it back into the pot in which it was cooked. Add the Parmesan cheese–butter mixture by spoonfuls, stirring until it has melted into a creamy sauce. Chuck in the asparagus, salt and pepper, and toss well so that the fettuccine is coated with the sauce. Serve immediately. Try not to swoon.

# Classic Spaghetti with Meatballs

serves 4

*A red-and-white checkered tablecloth. A wine bottle with a candle stuck in it. Spaghetti and meatballs. A Lady and the Tramp classic moment.*

2 tbsp. (30 ml) olive oil or vegetable oil
½ medium onion, chopped
2 cloves garlic, minced or pressed
½ medium sweet green pepper, chopped
½ cup (125 ml) sliced mushrooms
3 cups (750 ml) spaghetti sauce, homemade (see page 99) or prepared
    (you can use one 28 oz./796 ml jar or can)
½ tsp. (2 ml) dried oregano
½ tsp. (2 ml) dried basil (or 1 tbsp./15 ml chopped fresh basil)
1 batch Plain Old Meatballs, browned (see recipe on page 58)
Salt and black pepper, if needed
1 lb. (500 g) uncooked spaghetti
Grated Parmesan cheese for serving

In a large saucepan or Dutch oven, heat the oil over medium heat. Add the onion and garlic, and cook, stirring, for 3 to 5 minutes, until softened. Now add the green pepper and mushrooms, and cook for another 3 to 5 minutes. Add the spaghetti sauce, oregano and basil, and bring to a simmer.

Plunk the meatballs into the simmering sauce. Cover and cook, stirring often, for 20 to 30 minutes, or until the flavors are blended and the meatballs are tender. Taste, and add salt and pepper if you think it needs it.

Meanwhile, cook the pasta until tender but not mushy. Drain well and return it to the pot in which it was cooked. Add some of the sauce to moisten the pasta and stir well to mix. Spoon the rest of the sauce and the meatballs over each serving at the table. Sprinkle with Parmesan.

# Spicy Peanut Pasta with Chicken and Vegetables

serves 4

*Very delicious, totally addictive and super easy.*

## Peanut sauce

½ cup (125 ml) smooth peanut butter
½ cup (125 ml) hot water
2 tbsp. (30 ml) soy sauce
2 tbsp. (30 ml) cider vinegar or rice vinegar
2 tsp. (10 ml) sesame oil (if you have it)
¼ tsp. (1 ml) hot pepper flakes (or more, less or whatever)
2 cloves garlic

## Pasta, chicken, vegetables

1 lb. (500 g) thin spaghetti or Asian noodles
1 tbsp. (15 ml) vegetable oil
1 lb. (500 g) boneless, skinless chicken breasts, cut into ½-inch (1 cm) cubes
2 tsp. (10 ml) finely chopped fresh gingerroot
2 cups (500 ml) mixed stir-fry vegetables, fresh or frozen (broccoli florets, snow
   peas, sweet peppers, mushrooms, whatever you like)
2 green onions, sliced
2 tbsp. (30 ml) chopped peanuts, salted or unsalted

First, make the peanut sauce. In a blender or food processor, combine the peanut butter, water, soy sauce, vinegar, sesame oil, hot pepper flakes and garlic. Blend until smooth. Set aside.

Cook the pasta in boiling salted water until tender but not mushy. Scoop out about 1 cup (250 ml) of the pasta-cooking water and reserve, then drain the pasta thoroughly and rinse under cold running water. Set aside.

Heat the oil in a large skillet over high heat. Add the cubed chicken and stir-fry until lightly browned — 6 to 8 minutes. Remove the chicken to a bowl, leaving as much of the oil behind in the pan as possible. Add the mixed vegetables and the gingerroot, and

### Shrimp? Pork? Why not?

Sure — go ahead and substitute 1 lb. (500 g) shelled shrimp or thinly sliced pork for the chicken in this recipe. Use what you have and what you like — it's all good!

cook, stirring constantly, just until the vegetables are tender but still crisp. Return the chicken to the pan along with the pasta and toss to combine. Add the peanut sauce, stir to mix, then cook just until the sauce is heated through. If the peanut sauce seems a bit too thick, you can add some of the reserved pasta-cooking water to thin the sauce so that everything is nicely coated and not at all gummy.

Sprinkle with green onions and chopped peanuts and serve immediately.

# Single-Skillet Spaghetti serves 4

*You've got to love a recipe that leaves you only a spoon and a single frying pan to wash.*

1 lb. (500 g) lean ground beef, ground turkey or ground chicken
2 cups (500 ml) sliced mushrooms
1 medium onion, chopped
1 medium sweet green pepper, chopped
1 can (28 oz./796 ml) diced tomatoes
1 cup (250 ml) water
1½ cups (375 ml) broken uncooked spaghetti
1 tsp. (5 ml) dried oregano
1 tsp. (5 ml) salt
¼ tsp. (1 ml) black pepper
2 cups (500 ml) shredded cheese (mozzarella, cheddar or whatever you have)

In a large skillet, combine the ground meat, mushrooms, onions and green pepper. Cook over medium-high heat until the meat is browned and the vegetables are softened — 10 to 12 minutes.

Dump in the tomatoes, water, uncooked spaghetti, oregano, salt and pepper. Bring to a boil, then reduce the heat to medium low. Cover, and cook for 15 to 20 minutes, stirring occasionally, or until the spaghetti is tender. Remove from heat, stir in the cheese and serve.

# Perfect Pesto Sauce

*Get your hands on a big bunch of fresh basil and make a batch of this wonderful stuff to use right now or stash away in the freezer. It's a summer miracle!*

¼ cup (60 ml) pine nuts (you can substitute almonds or walnuts, but the flavor
   will be different)
2 cups (500 ml) fresh basil leaves, rinsed, dried and firmly packed in measuring cup
½ cup (125 ml) olive oil
2 cloves garlic (or more, if you're that kind of person)
½ tsp. (2 ml) salt
¾ cup (175 ml) freshly grated Parmesan cheese

Place the pine nuts into a small skillet over low heat. Toast them very gently, stirring constantly, for 3 to 5 minutes, or until the nuts are lightly browned. Watch this like a hawk because you do not want to burn them. (Pine nuts are crazy expensive.) Set aside to cool.

Cram the basil leaves, olive oil, toasted pine nuts, garlic and salt into the container of a food processor or blender. Blend until almost smooth, scraping the sides down several times so that the mixture blends evenly. A little texture is okay — but no big leafy clumps. Add the Parmesan cheese and blend briefly just to mix.

Makes 1 cup (250 ml) Perfect Pesto, enough to sauce 1 lb. (500 g) cooked pasta or about 4 servings.

## How to pesto properly

Wait! Don't just glop all that pesto over your cooked pasta! A proper pesto pasta should be light and creamy. Here's how to do it right.

Before draining your pasta, remove a cupful of pasta cooking water from the pot and set it aside. Drain the pasta in a colander and transfer it to a bowl. Add the pesto, a spoonful at a time, alternating with a drizzle of pasta-cooking water. Toss until the pasta is very lightly sauced. The pasta water thins the sauce slightly to give the pesto a luscious, creamy consistency. Perfectly proper.

## Other pestobilities

- Whisk into Basic Vinaigrette Dressing (see recipe on page 48) for a pesto vinaigrette.
- Dab it onto toasted baguette slices and top with a sliver of sun-dried tomato or sliced fresh mozzarella cheese.
- Add a spoonful to Minestrone Soup (see recipe on page 36) before serving.
- Mix together equal amounts of pesto, yogurt and mayonnaise for a delicious dip.

# Penne with Roasted Vegetables serves 4–6

*Knock everyone's socks off with this fabulous vegetarian pasta dish. I mean, who needs socks, right?*

3 cups (750 ml) cherry or grape tomatoes

2 medium onions, cut into 1-inch (2 cm) chunks

2 medium sweet green or red peppers, seeded and cut into 1-inch (2 cm) chunks

1 medium zucchini, cut into 1-inch (2 cm) chunks

⅓ cup (75 ml) olive oil

¼ cup (60 ml) black olives, pitted and chopped

¼ cup (60 ml) fresh parsley, chopped

¼ cup (60 ml) fresh basil, chopped

1 tbsp. (15 ml) capers, drained (if you have them)

2 cloves garlic, minced or pressed

1 tsp. (5 ml) salt

¼ tsp. (1 ml) black pepper

1 lb. (500 g) uncooked penne pasta (about 5 cups/1.25 liters)

⅓ cup (75 ml) grated Parmesan cheese (plus more for sprinkling at the table)

Preheat the oven to 425°F (220°C). Have ready two rimmed cookie sheets.

Toss the tomatoes, onions, peppers and zucchini in a large bowl with the olive oil and spread them out in a single layer on the cookie sheets.

Place in the preheated oven and roast, undisturbed, for 30 to 40 minutes, or until the vegetables are starting to brown and the tomatoes have collapsed. Remove from the oven and transfer to a bowl.

Add the olives, parsley, basil, capers (if using), garlic, salt and pepper. Toss gently to combine, then set aside.

Cook the penne pasta in plenty of boiling salted water until tender but not mushy. Drain, then return the penne to the pot in which it was cooked. Add the vegetable mixture, place the pot over medium heat and let everything heat through for just a minute or two, tossing gently to combine (but don't mush it all up).

Stir in the Parmesan cheese and serve with additional Parmesan for sprinkling at the table.

# Macaroni and Cheese Not from a Box

*Yes, there are times when you want macaroni and cheese from a box — neon orange, artificially flavored and very fast. But then there are times when you want the other kind. The kind with lots of real cheese and a crunchy top. The kind that takes more than seven minutes to make. This is it. And it is good.*

3 cups (750 ml) uncooked elbow macaroni (or other medium-size pasta shape)
1 *double* recipe Basic White Sauce (see recipe on page 107)
3 cups (750 ml) grated sharp cheddar cheese
1 cup (30 ml) fresh bread crumbs
2 tbsp. (30 ml) butter, melted
Additional salt and pepper, to taste

Preheat the oven to 350°F (180°C). Grease a 9 x 13-inch (23 x 33 cm) rectangular baking dish (or a baking dish that holds 2 or 3 quarts/liters).

Cook the macaroni in a large pot of boiling salted water until tender but not mushy. Drain thoroughly and rinse with cold water to stop any further cooking. Return the cooked macaroni to the pot. Set aside off the heat.

While the macaroni is cooking, make a *double* recipe of white sauce. (Just double all the amounts of the ingredients in the sauce recipe — cooking time will be a little longer.) When the sauce has thickened, remove the pot from the heat and stir in the grated cheese, mixing until the cheese is completely melted and the sauce is smooth. Taste, and add additional salt and pepper if you think it needs it.

Combine the cheese sauce with the cooked macaroni and stir until mixed. Transfer to the prepared baking dish.

Mix the bread crumbs with the melted butter and sprinkle this on top of the macaroni. Place in the preheated oven and bake for 30 to 40 minutes, or until the sauce is bubbly and the topping is crisp and golden. You can, if you must, eat this with ketchup.

## Basic White Sauce

This is an essential recipe. Memorize it and you will look like a Food Network star. It has a million uses — mixed with cheese as a base for Macaroni and Cheese (see recipe opposite), or with some chopped fresh herbs or garlic to pour over steamed fresh broccoli.

2 tbsp. (30 ml) butter
2 tbsp. (30 ml) all-purpose flour
1 cup (250 ml) milk
½ tsp. (2 ml) salt
¼ tsp. (1 ml) black pepper (or white pepper, if you prefer)

Melt the butter in a small saucepan over medium heat. Stir in the flour, mixing well. Cook very gently for a minute or two, stirring constantly. Now very slowly whisk in the milk. At first the mixture will be lumpy, but as you stir it over the heat, it will become smooth and begin to thicken as it comes to a simmer. Continue cooking the sauce over low heat for 3 to 5 minutes longer, whisking constantly so that it doesn't stick to the bottom of the saucepan and burn.

Season with salt and pepper. If you want to use herbs, add them now. If you want to add cheese, remove the pot from the heat and stir in the cheese (about ½ cup/125 ml) mixing until the sauce is smooth and the cheese is melted. Don't cook the sauce after you've added the cheese — it may become stringy.

Makes about 1 cup (250 ml) white sauce.

# Crazy Good Lasagna serves 8

*Oven-ready, no-boil lasagna noodles make this almost too easy to be believed. And if you cook the sauce ahead of time, you can throw this lasagna together in nothing flat. That's crazy!*

1 recipe sauce (see recipe below)
2 cups (500 ml) ricotta cheese
2 eggs, lightly beaten
2 tbsp. (30 ml) chopped fresh parsley
3 cups (750 ml) grated mozzarella cheese
¼ cup (60 ml) grated Parmesan cheese
15 oven-ready lasagna noodles

Preheat the oven to 350°F (180°C). Grease a 9 x 13-inch (23 x 33 cm) rectangular baking dish.

In a bowl, mix the ricotta cheese with the eggs and parsley.

Spread about 1 cup (250 ml) of the sauce on the bottom of the prepared baking dish — it won't quite cover the bottom, but that's okay. Arrange 5 of the lasagna noodles on the sauce, covering the entire bottom of the baking dish as much as possible. If you need to break some of the noodles to make it fit properly, go ahead and do that. No one will ever know. Spread 2 cups (500 ml) of the sauce over the noodles, then spoon half the ricotta mixture over the sauce (dollop it as evenly as you can). Sprinkle with 1 cup (250 ml) of mozzarella cheese. Repeat: 5 more noodles, 2 cups (500 ml) sauce, the rest of the ricotta and another cup (250 ml) mozzarella. Are you still with me?

Finally, put the last 5 lasagna noodles on top, spread the rest of the sauce over them, then sprinkle with the remaining mozzarella and all the Parmesan cheese. Whew!

Cover the baking dish loosely with foil (tent the foil up a little so that it doesn't touch the cheese), place it in the preheated oven and bake for 30 minutes. Remove the foil and bake for another 15 to 20 minutes, or until the sauce is bubbling and the lasagna noodles are tender (poke a knife into the middle to make sure).

## Sauce
Sauté 1 cup (250 ml) each chopped mushrooms and diced zucchini in a bit of olive oil until tender. Add to 4 cups (1 liter) spaghetti sauce (homemade or store-bought) along with 2 cups (500 ml) raw chopped fresh spinach.

# Spaghetti Carbonara

*This pasta dish cooks in the time it takes to boil the spaghetti — it's much more than the sum of its very humble ingredients.*

2 eggs, beaten
½ cup (125 ml) grated Parmesan cheese
½ lb. (250 g) uncooked spaghetti
6 slices bacon, chopped
½ tsp. (2 ml) hot pepper flakes (optional, but good)
½ tsp. (2 ml) salt
¼ tsp. (1 ml) black pepper

Put a large pot of salted water on high heat and bring to a boil.

While the water is heating, stir together the beaten eggs and the Parmesan cheese in a large bowl, then set it aside. This dish comes together quickly and you won't have time to mess around once you begin cooking.

When the water boils, stir in the spaghetti.

While the spaghetti is cooking, place the bacon in a small skillet over medium heat. Add the red pepper flakes and cook, stirring often, until the bacon is crisp. Set this aside until the spaghetti is cooked.

When the spaghetti is tender but not mushy, scoop out about 1/2 cup (125 ml) of the cooking water (you'll need it in a minute), then drain the pasta well. Dump it immediately into the bowl with the eggs and Parmesan cheese and stir. Add the bacon and the fat from the pan, and just enough of the reserved cooking water to make a creamy sauce. The hot spaghetti actually cooks the eggs, and the whole thing combines into a delicious sauce you'd never in a million years guess was made in about a minute. Season with salt and pepper and serve right away — pronto.

This recipe makes only 2 servings but can easily be doubled to serve more people.

# Pizza

You can make any of these pizzas with either homemade dough (Italian Everything Dough, see recipe on page 159) or store-bought fresh pizza dough. If you're in a big hurry and just want a pizza *immediately right now this minute*, see sidebar on page 113 for other perfectly pleasant pizza crust possibilities.

# Pizza with Tomato Sauce and Whatever

*Classic pizza — like your favorite takeout, only better.*

½ recipe Italian Everything Dough (see recipe on page 159), store-bought pizza dough or other crust (see sidebar on page 113)
1 cup (250 ml) Big Batch Spaghetti Sauce (see recipe on page 99) or store-bought tomato pasta sauce
2 cups (500 ml) shredded mozzarella cheese
Additional toppings — as many as you like

Preheat the oven to 450°F (230°C). Grease a 12-inch (30 cm) pizza pan (a cookie sheet will do if you don't have an official pizza pan). Sprinkle the pan with cornmeal.

If you're using homemade (or store-bought) pizza dough, roll it out on a well-floured surface to a 12-inch (30 cm) round. Transfer to the prepared pan and pinch the edges up to form a bit of a ridge all around.

Spread the pasta sauce evenly over the crust in the baking pan to about 1/2 inch (1 cm) from the edge. Sprinkle with the shredded mozzarella cheese, then top with whatever toppings you want to use (see sidebar for a million ideas).

Place in the preheated oven and bake for 18 to 20 minutes, until the cheese is bubbling and the crust is browned when you peek underneath.

Makes one 12-inch (30 cm) pizza or 3 to 4 servings. Or less.

## Toppings, toppings and more toppings

- bacon, partly cooked and chopped up
- pepperoni, of course
- ham or prosciutto, chopped
- grated Parmesan cheese
- other cheeses — like Swiss or Asiago or provolone
- sliced fresh mushrooms
- anchovies!
- chopped green or red sweet peppers
- diced or sliced fresh tomatoes
- grilled eggplant or zucchini slices
- baby spinach leaves
- chopped sun-dried tomatoes
- torn fresh basil leaves
- broccoli florets
- chopped roasted red peppers
- chopped fresh hot peppers or pickled hot peppers
- chopped or sliced marinated artichoke hearts
- sliced green or black olives
- baby arugula leaves
- halved bocconcini cheese
- thinly sliced potatoes
- pineapple chunks (to each his own)

# Pizza with Pesto, Goat Cheese and Sun-Dried Tomatoes

serves 3–4

*Make your own pesto sauce (see page 104) or use store-bought for this deliciously different pizza. You may never go back to tomato sauce again.*

½ recipe Italian Everything Dough (see recipe on page 159), store-bought pizza dough or other crust (see sidebar opposite)

1 cup (250 ml) pesto sauce, homemade (see recipe on page 104) or store-bought

½ cup (125 ml) sun-dried tomatoes packed in oil, drained and cut into strips

5 oz. (140 g) goat cheese, plain or with herbs, crumbled (about 1 cup/250 ml)

## Old pizza maker's trick

Sauce first, then cheese, then veggies on top of the cheese. This allows the steam from the vegetables to escape and prevents sogginess.

Preheat the oven to 450°F (230°C). Grease a 12-inch (30 cm) pizza pan (a cookie sheet will do if you don't have an official pizza pan). Sprinkle the pan with cornmeal.

On a well-floured surface, roll out the dough to a 12-inch (30 cm) round. Transfer to the prepared pan and pinch the edges up to form a bit of a ridge. Spread the pesto sauce evenly over the prepared pizza crust to about 1/2 inch (1 cm) from the edge. Sprinkle with the sun-dried tomatoes and top with crumbled goat cheese.

Bake in the preheated oven for 18 to 20 minutes, until the pesto is sizzling and the crust is browned when you peek underneath.

Makes one 12-inch (30 cm) pizza or 3 to 4 servings. Or less.

## Do-it-yourself frozen pizza

If you're already making a batch of Italian Everything Dough, why not make two pizzas and freeze the extra one for a rainy day? Here's how to do it.

Assemble the prepared, unbaked pizza on a pan and place it in the freezer — don't wrap it or anything. Let the pizza freeze solid, then lift it from the pan and wrap it tightly in foil or plastic. The toppings won't stick to the wrap once they're frozen. Store in the freezer until you're ready to use it.

To bake, remove pizza from the freezer and unwrap. Place on a lightly greased pan and bake at 450°F (230°C) for 25 to 30 minutes, or until done the way you like it. Aren't you clever?

# Pizza with Caramelized Onions and Pine Nuts

*Sweet caramelized onions, ricotta cheese, crunchy pine nuts. This is one fabulous pizza. Prepare to be amazed.*

1 tbsp. (15 ml) olive oil
1 tbsp. (15 ml) butter
3 medium onions, thinly sliced
2 tbsp. (30 ml) balsamic vinegar
1 tbsp. (15 ml) granulated sugar
½ tsp. (2 ml) salt
½ recipe Italian Everything Dough (see
    recipe on page 159), store-bought pizza
    dough or other crust (see sidebar)
½ cup (125 ml) ricotta cheese
¼ cup (60 ml) grated Parmesan cheese
2 tbsp. (30 ml) pine nuts

## Potential pizza crust alternatives

- pita bread
- naan bread
- flour tortilla
- English muffin
- French or Italian bread
- prepared prebaked pizza crust
- puff pastry dough
- sliced cooked polenta (from a tube)
- a flat omelet

First, make the caramelized onions. Heat the olive oil and butter (you can use all olive oil, if you prefer) in a large skillet over medium-low heat. Add the sliced onions and cook, stirring occasionally, until the onions turn a deep golden brown, about 30 minutes. Add the balsamic vinegar, sugar and salt, and cook for 5 minutes, until the liquid has almost completely evaporated. Let cool.

Preheat the oven to 450°F (230°C). Grease a 12-inch (30 cm) pizza pan (a cookie sheet will do if you don't have an official pizza pan). Sprinkle the pan with cornmeal.

On a well-floured surface, roll out the dough to a 12-inch (30 cm) round. Transfer to the prepared pan and pinch the edges up to form a bit of a ridge around the edge.

Mix together the ricotta and the Parmesan cheese in a small bowl. Spread it as evenly as possible over the prepared pizza crust to about 1/2 inch (1 cm) from the edge. Spread the onions over the cheese, then sprinkle with the pine nuts.

Bake in the preheated oven for about 18 to 20 minutes, until the top is sizzling and the crust is browned when you peek underneath.

Makes 3 to 4 servings. Or maybe just one …

# Vehemently Vegetarian

## Going Vegetarian

There are plenty of very sensible reasons to go vegetarian, a few poor ones and even some reasons not to consider it at all. Becoming a vegetarian isn't rocket science, but it does require some understanding of your nutritional needs and an open mind. All you have to do is follow the basic nutritional guidelines on page 10, learn to cook a thing or two and, oh yeah, you really do have to like vegetables. Not a problem.

# Vaguely Chinese Stir-Fry serves 2–3

The secret to a quick and easy stir-fry is to have every single thing prepared before you start cooking so that you're not madly slicing or measuring in mid stir. The prep takes a little time, but the actual cooking is done in minutes. This recipe is infinitely variable — see page 116 for some ideas.

3 tbsp. (45 ml) vegetable oil, divided
8 oz. (250 g) firm tofu, cut into ½-inch (1 cm) cubes (about 1½ cups/375 ml cubes)
1 bunch broccoli, florets cut apart, stems thinly sliced
1 medium sweet green or red pepper, cut into 1-inch (2 cm) squares
2 cloves garlic, minced or pressed
4 green onions, halved lengthwise and cut into 1-inch (2 cm) pieces
1 cup (250 ml) vegetable broth, divided (prepared broth or made from bouillon cubes or powder)
3 tbsp. (45 ml) soy sauce
1 tbsp. (15 ml) cornstarch
1 tsp. (5 ml) sesame oil
¼ cup (60 ml) cashews or peanuts (cashews are really better)

Arrange all the cut-up vegetables separately on a large platter or separate bowls so that you can add each type to the stir-fry individually. Cut up the tofu and have it ready. In a small bowl, stir together 1/4 cup (60 ml) of the broth, the soy sauce, cornstarch and sesame oil, and set it aside. Have the garlic minced and the cashews measured. Okay. Now you're ready to start cooking.

Pour about half of the oil into a wok or large skillet and heat it over high heat. Toss in the tofu pieces and stir-fry until very lightly browned. Transfer the browned tofu to a bowl and set aside.

Add the rest of the oil to the wok or skillet and heat until a drop of water sizzles when it hits the pan. Add the broccoli and pepper, and stir-fry for 1 or 2 minutes, or until well mixed and glossy with oil. Toss in the green onions and the garlic, stir, then add the remaining 1/4 cup (60 ml) of broth. Slam a cover on the pan and let the vegetables steam for a minute or two, until the broccoli is bright green and starting to become tender. Remove the lid, toss the tofu back into the pan and give it a good stir. Add the soy sauce mixture, stirring constantly. The sauce will thicken and become glossy. Sprinkle the cashews or peanuts over the top and serve immediately with hot cooked rice or noodles.

## Variations on a stir-fry (vegetarian and non-)

Switch up or add to the veggies, depending on what is available. Snow peas, bean sprouts, thinly sliced carrots, mushrooms, asparagus are all great stir-fry candidates. And some Asian chili paste or chopped fresh ginger or chilies are great if you want to amp up the flavour.

- Non-vegetarians can add cubed chicken, shelled shrimp or thinly sliced beef or pork instead of or in addition to the tofu.
- No tofu? No meat? How about an egg? Scramble an egg or two for a shot of protein.
- Leftover pasta — noodles, spaghetti, linguine — are all great in a stir-fry. Add at the end and toss to heat through.

## Tofu (oh come on, just try it)

Look, it's not made from pond slime or fish livers or anything weird like that. Tofu is a nice, wholesome food made from perfectly harmless soybeans. It's cheap, packed with protein and low in fat. It doesn't taste like much on its own but absorbs the flavor of whatever it hangs out with. Try it in a few different ways to see what you like.

**Bake it!** Buy extra-firm tofu, cut it into sticks or slabs, douse it with barbecue sauce and bake until sizzling. Or cut extra-firm tofu into fingers, dip in beaten egg and bread crumbs and bake on an oiled cookie sheet until crisp (great with ketchup).

**Stir-fry it!** Marinate ½-inch (1 cm) cubes of firm tofu in soy sauce before stir-frying with veggies. Throw in a spoonful of Asian chili paste or sriracha. Amazing!

**Freeze it!** Stash a couple of blocks of tofu in the freezer and let them freeze solid, then thaw them out. The texture changes completely. You can now crumble the tofu (as a substitute for ground meat) or slice it into slivers to throw into a stir-fry.

**Go naked!** The tofu, that is. Just float a few cubes in your soup or toss some into your salad. (Mostly recommended for already-committed tofu lovers.)

# Simple Lentil Dal

*Dal is an Indian dish, usually made with lentils or other legumes. It tends to be soupy and goes very well with rice as part of an Indian meal. You can even roll it into a warm flour tortilla for a quick meal on the run. Adjust the spiciness to suit your taste.*

1 cup (250 ml) dried brown or green lentils
3 cups (750 ml) water
1 tsp. (5 ml) salt
2 tbsp. (30 ml) grated fresh gingerroot
2 tsp. (10 ml) curry powder
2 tbsp. (30 ml) vegetable oil
½ tsp. (2 ml) hot pepper flakes (or to taste)
½ tsp. (2 ml) ground cumin
2 tbsp. (30 ml) chopped cilantro
2 tbsp. (30 ml) lemon juice

Pick over the lentils (remove any small stones or other non-lentil objects) and rinse them well. Place in a medium saucepan and add the water and salt. Bring to a boil over medium heat, then reduce the heat to low, cover the pot and let simmer for 30 to 45 minutes, stirring occasionally.

Add the grated ginger and the curry powder, and continue to simmer for another 10 to 15 minutes, or until the lentils are completely soft. The mixture should be like a thick soup — if it's getting too dry, add a bit more water, 1/4 cup (60 ml) at a time.

Meanwhile, heat the oil in a small skillet over medium heat. Add the hot pepper flakes and cumin, and cook, stirring, for 2 or 3 minutes. Add to the lentils in the pot, along with the chopped cilantro and lemon juice, and stir to mix. Done.

Serve with rice or bread or alongside Potato and Pea Curry (see recipe on page 119).

# Potato Paprikash

*Who says you can't have potatoes for dinner? Add a salad and you've made yourself a two-course meal.*

¼ cup (60 ml) olive oil or vegetable oil
2 medium onions, chopped
6 large potatoes, sliced ¼ inch (.5 cm) thick (6 to 8 cups sliced potatoes)
1 tbsp. (15 ml) paprika
1 tsp. (5 ml) dried thyme
½ tsp. (2 ml) salt
¼ tsp. (1 ml) black pepper
2 cups (500 ml) water or vegetable broth (prepared broth or made from
    bouillon cubes or powder)
Sour cream or plain Greek yogurt for serving

Heat the oil in a large skillet over medium heat. Add the onions and sauté for about 5 minutes, or until softened. Add the potatoes, stir them around a little, then sprinkle with the paprika, thyme, salt and pepper. Cook for 2 minutes, then pour in the liquid — it should just about cover the potatoes (adjust the amount of liquid accordingly). Slam the lid on the pan, reduce the heat to medium low, bring to a simmer and let cook for 15 to 20 minutes, or until the potatoes are tender when poked with a fork. Serve with a dollop of sour cream or yogurt, if desired.

Makes 2 servings as a main dish, about 4 servings as a side dish.

## Paprikash alternatives — vegetarian and otherwise

Non-vegetarians can add 2 cups (500 ml) smoked sausage, kielbasa or hot dogs, cut into 1-inch (2 cm) pieces, to the pan when they sauté the onions. This turns the dish into Sausage and Potato Paprikash, a Hungarian classic. Sort of.

Sprinkle the dish with cheese — shredded cheddar or Swiss or crumbled feta — when it's just about ready to serve. Cover and remove from heat. Let sit just until the cheese is melted.

Toss a diced block of tofu in with the onions to boost the protein content. The tofu will blend deliciously with the potatoes and paprika sauce.

118   *Vehemently Vegetarian*

# Potato and Pea Curry

*Add a bowl of chutney, some sliced cucumbers and some warm pita or naan bread. Or serve this with Simple Lentil Dal (see recipe on page 117) for a full-on Indian dinner. Your karma will thank you.*

6 medium potatoes, cut into ½-inch (1 cm) cubes
2 tbsp. (30 ml) vegetable oil
1 tsp. (5 ml) whole mustard seeds
2 medium onions, chopped
1 tbsp. (15 ml) curry powder
¼ tsp. (1 ml) cayenne pepper (or as much as you like)
1 cup (250 ml) frozen peas
1 tsp. (5 ml) salt
1 cup (250 ml) water
¼ cup (60 ml) chopped cilantro or parsley

Cook the potatoes in a steamer basket set over boiling water, or in a pot of boiling water, until tender but still just a little firm in the middle (poke with a fork to be sure). Drain and set aside while you prepare the rest of the ingredients.

Heat the oil in a large skillet over medium heat. Add the mustard seeds — enjoy the show as they crackle and pop in the pan — then add the onions when the popping has died down. Cook, stirring, for 7 to 10 minutes, or until the onions start to brown. Add the curry powder and cayenne, stir to mix, then add the cooked potatoes, peas, salt and water. Reduce the heat to low, cover the skillet and cook curry for about 5 minutes, or until flavors have gotten acquainted with one another. Sprinkle with cilantro or parsley and continue to cook for another 10 minutes, until potatoes are completely tender. If the curry gets too dry, you can add a few spoonfuls of water as the dish cooks — it should stay moist but not soupy.

# Eggplant Parmigiana

*Every vegetarian needs a few recipes to haul out when carnivores (your parents?)*
*come to dinner. This is a good one. So delicious and satisfying — who needs meat?*

½ cup (125 ml) olive oil or vegetable oil
2 eggs
½ cup (125 ml) milk
2 cups (200 ml) dry bread crumbs
1 tsp. (5 ml) dried oregano
½ tsp. (2 ml) salt
¼ tsp. (1 ml) black pepper
2 medium eggplants
4 cups (1 liter) spaghetti sauce, homemade (see page 99) or prepared sauce
    from a jar or can
½ cup (125 ml) grated Parmesan cheese
3 cups (750 ml) shredded mozzarella cheese

Preheat the oven to 425°F (220°C). Brush a rimmed cookie sheet with some of
the oil. Grease a 9 x 13-inch (23 x 33 cm) rectangular baking dish.

In a small dish, beat the eggs with the milk. In another dish, combine the bread
crumbs, oregano, salt and pepper.

Without peeling them, slice the eggplants crosswise into 1/4-inch (0.5 cm) thick
slices. Working with 1 slice at a time, dip first into the egg mixture, then into
the bread crumb mixture, turning to coat both sides. When all the slices are
breaded, arrange as many as will fit in a single layer on the prepared cookie
sheet and drizzle with a little more of the oil. (Don't crowd the slices — you'll
need to bake them in 2 or 3 batches.) Place in the oven and bake for 20 to 25
minutes, turning over the slices halfway through the baking time, until lightly
browned on both sides. Remove from oven and repeat until all the eggplant
slices are done. Set them aside.

Reduce the oven temperature to 350°F (180°C).

Spread 1/2 cup (125 ml) of the spaghetti sauce on the bottom of the prepared
baking dish (this is just a thin layer). On this, arrange a layer of eggplant slices,
cutting them, if necessary, to cover the bottom of the dish. Spread with 1 cup
(250 ml) of the spaghetti sauce, sprinkle with some of the Parmesan cheese
and about 1 cup (250 ml) of the mozzarella cheese. Repeat — another layer of
eggplant, another cup of spaghetti sauce, a sprinkle of Parmesan and a cup of

mozzarella. Finish with the remaining eggplant slices, all the rest of the spaghetti sauce and the rest of the Parmesan cheese. Reserve the remaining 1 cup (250 ml) of mozzarella — you'll need it later.

Place the dish in the preheated oven and bake for 30 minutes. Now sprinkle with the reserved mozzarella and bake for another 15 minutes, or until the dish is bubbling and the cheese is gooey and melted.

# Chunky Vegetable Stew serves 4–6

*Here's a substantial vegetarian stew that will warm your innards on a chilly evening. This is great spooned over rice, couscous, quinoa or pasta.*

2 tbsp. (30 ml) olive oil or vegetable oil
2 medium onions, cut into large chunks
2 cups (500 ml) cauliflower florets
2 medium potatoes, cut into 1-inch (2 cm) cubes (about 2 cups/500 ml cubes)
1 large sweet potato, peeled and cut into 1-inch (2 cm) cubes
    (about 1½ cups/375 ml cubes)
2 cups (500 ml) mushrooms, halved or quartered
4 cloves garlic, minced or pressed
1½ cups (375 ml) diced tomatoes, canned or fresh
1½ cups (375 ml) vegetable broth (prepared broth or made from
    bouillon cubes or powder)
1 can (19 oz./540 ml) lentils, drained and rinsed
½ tsp. (2 ml) hot pepper flakes, if desired
1 tsp. (5 ml) salt
¼ tsp. (1 ml) black pepper
2 cups (500 ml) raw spinach, roughly torn up

Heat the oil in a large pot or Dutch oven over medium heat. Add the onions and cook, stirring, for 3 or 4 minutes, until the onions begin to soften. Add the cauliflower, potato and sweet potato, and cook for about 10 minutes, stirring occasionally. Add the mushrooms and garlic, and cook for 5 minutes. Add the tomatoes, vegetable broth, lentils, hot pepper flakes, salt and black pepper, and bring to a boil. Cover the pot with a lid, reduce the heat to medium low and continue to cook for about 20 minutes, or until all the vegetables are tender. Toss in the spinach leaves, cover the pot and cook for just a minute or two. Serve.

# Oven-Roasted Carrot and Sweet Potato Casserole

serves 6–8

*A little sweet, a little exotic — this dish turns humble root vegetables and a can of chickpeas into a wonderful dinner.*

4 medium onions, sliced

3 tbsp. (45 ml) olive oil or vegetable oil, divided

1 can (19 oz./540 ml) chickpeas, drained and rinsed

4 medium carrots, peeled or scrubbed and cut into ½-inch (1 cm) chunks

4 medium sweet potatoes, peeled and cut into ½-inch (1 cm) chunks

½ cup (125 ml) vegetable broth, homemade or store-bought
   (canned or from bouillon cubes or powder)

¼ cup (60 ml) raisins

¼ cup (60 ml) granulated sugar or brown sugar

½ tsp. (2 cm) cinnamon

½ tsp. (2 ml) salt

¼ tsp. (1 ml) black pepper

chopped fresh parsley or cilantro for garnish, if desired

Preheat the oven to 400°F (200°C). Grease a 9 x 13-inch (23 x 33 cm) rectangular baking dish.

In a large skillet, sauté the onions in 2 tbsp. (30 ml) of the oil for 6 to 8 minutes, until softened and beginning to turn golden. Spread evenly in the prepared baking dish. Sprinkle the chickpeas over the onions.

In a large bowl, toss together the carrots, sweet potatoes, broth, raisins, sugar, cinnamon, salt, pepper and the remaining 1 tbsp. (15 ml) oil. Mix well, then dump this over the chickpeas and spread the mixture out evenly.

Place in the preheated oven and bake for 35 to 45 minutes, basting the top occasionally with some of the juices from the bottom of the baking dish, until the vegetables are tender and browned. Sprinkle with a little chopped parsley or cilantro before serving, if you want.

This is wonderful with couscous or lemony rice (see pages 148 and 149).

# Chock Full of Veggies Chili

serves 8

*This chili is loaded with veggies, nice and thick, and just spicy enough to make you sit up and take notice.*

1 large eggplant, cut into ½-inch (1 cm) cubes
2½ tsp. (12 ml) salt, divided
¼ cup (60 ml) olive oil or vegetable oil
2 medium onions, chopped
2 medium zucchini, cut into ½-inch (1 cm) cubes
2 medium red or green sweet peppers, chopped
4 cloves garlic, minced or pressed
1 can (28 oz./796 ml) diced tomatoes (or 4 cups/1 liter chopped fresh
   tomatoes)
3 tbsp. (45 ml) Mexican chili powder
1 tbsp. (15 ml) cumin
1 tbsp. (15 ml) dried oregano
1 tsp. (5 ml) black pepper
½ tsp. (2 ml) cayenne pepper (or more, or less, to taste)
1 can (19 oz./540 ml) kidney, black or pinto beans, drained
1½ cups (375 ml) corn kernels, frozen, canned or cut from the cob

Place the eggplant cubes in a colander set over a bowl and toss with 2 tsp. (10 ml) of the salt. Let sit for about 1 hour to drain, then rinse and pat dry with paper towel. Salting the eggplant removes some of the liquid and helps it cook more evenly. If you don't have the time for this kind of fussing around, you can skip this step.

Heat the oil in a large pot or Dutch oven over medium heat. Add the onions, zucchini, peppers and garlic, and cook for 8 to 10 minutes, until everything has begun to soften. Add the eggplant cubes and continue to cook, stirring occasionally, for 8 to 10 minutes longer, until the vegetables are tender.

Add the tomatoes, chili powder, cumin, oregano, black pepper, cayenne and the remaining salt, and bring the mixture to a boil. Lower the heat, cover the pot and cook the veggie chili gently, stirring once in a while, for about 15 minutes.

Add the beans and corn, and cook for another 15 minutes. Taste, and adjust the seasoning if necessary.

Serve hot, sprinkled with cheese if you like, and accompanied by rice or a big ol' hunk of Corn Bread (see page 158 for recipe).

# Chickenless Fingers

*Great kid food — or adult food, for that matter. Don't forget the dipping sauce!*

1 pkg. (12 oz./350 g) extra-firm tofu
½ cup (125 ml) dry bread crumbs
¼ tsp. (1 ml) salt
¼ tsp. (1 ml) black pepper
¼ tsp. (1 ml) dried oregano
¼ tsp. (1 ml) garlic powder
¼ cup (60 ml) all-purpose flour
1 egg, beaten
Your favorite dipping sauces

Preheat the oven to 375°F (190°C). Grease a cookie sheet.

Cut the block of tofu into fingers about 1/2 inch (1 cm) thick and 3 inches (8 cm) long, more or less.

In a small bowl, combine the bread crumbs, salt, pepper, oregano and garlic powder. Place the flour in another small bowl. Have the beaten egg ready in a third bowl.

First, roll the tofu fingers in the flour, then dip each one into the beaten egg and then the bread crumb mixture to coat. (The flour helps bind the egg and crumbs to the tofu so that the crumbs don't just fall off.)

Place breaded fingers on the prepared cookie sheet and bake in the preheated oven for about 30 minutes, turning them over halfway through.

Serve the Chickenless Fingers hot with an assortment of dipping sauces: ketchup, sweet and sour, plum sauce, barbecue sauce, sweet chili sauce, hot mustard, whatever.

Makes about 16 fingers.

## They're everywhere! They're everywhere!

If you're a vegetarian yourself or you want to cook a vegetarian meal, you'll find many recipes throughout this book that contain no meat. Many of the pasta recipes, pizzas, appetizers and soups are either already vegetarian or can easily be adapted by omitting meat or substituting vegetarian ingredients for meat-based ones. So don't limit yourself to just this vegetarian chapter — vegetarian recipes are everywhere if you're looking for them!

# Eggs, Pancakes and Other Breakfast and Brunchy Things

But there's no law that says you can't have a scrambled egg for dinner or a plate of pancakes for lunch. So go ahead — be a rebel — we're perfectly okay with that.

# Extraordinary Eggs

Let's start with the basics. An egg is just about the easiest thing there is to cook. It's quick, cheap and nutritious, and always available everywhere. A simple boiled egg with toast can be a meal when you're hungry and in a hurry; or you can go all out and whip up a fancified omelet, filled with veggies and cheese. Let's start with the three most basic ways to prepare this miracle food.

# A Plain Boiled Egg

Place as many eggs as you want in a saucepan and add enough cold water to cover the eggs by about 1/2 inch (1 cm).

Place the pan over medium-high heat. As soon as the water reaches a boil, remove the pan from the burner and slam a lid on the pot. Begin timing:

- 1 minute for a very runny egg
- 4 minutes for a soft-boiled egg without any gooey spots
- 2 minutes for a soft-boiled egg
- 15 minutes for a hard-boiled egg

This method is guaranteed to give you a perfectly cooked egg that will not explode in the water. Put it in a nice eggy cup, sprinkle with a little salt and pepper, and eat it with your favorite Power Rangers spoon while you watch cartoons in your pajamas.

# Scrambled Eggs

Same eggs, two methods. Either way, it makes one serving.

2 eggs
1 tbsp. (15 ml) milk
2 tsp. (10 ml) butter

## Frying pan method

Crack the eggs into a bowl, add the milk and beat with a fork just until evenly yellow.

Melt the butter in a small frying pan over medium heat and cook until it gets foamy. When the foam subsides, pour in the eggs. Stir constantly with a fork or a wooden spoon until the eggs are almost set and scrambled the way you like them. Eggs will continue to cook for a minute or two after you remove the pan from the heat, so it's better to undercook them slightly.

## Microwave method

Measure the butter into a small microwave-safe dish and microwave it on high power for 15 to 20 seconds, until melted and hot.

Meanwhile, beat together the eggs and milk until evenly yellow. Add to the melted butter in the bowl. Cook on high power, stirring every 30 seconds, for 1 to 1 1/2 minutes, or until done the way you like them.

## A Perfect Flat Egg

Melt 1 tbsp. (15 ml) butter in a small frying pan over medium heat. Let it get foamy, and when the foam subsides, reduce the heat to low and very carefully crack in 1 egg. (*Do not* attempt to drop the egg into the pan from a great height, because the yolk will break and you will no longer have a *perfect* egg.) The egg will bubble and splatter a little, but it shouldn't be going berserk in the pan. If it is, turn the heat down a notch until the egg is just quietly sizzling.

Let your egg continue to cook over low heat until you begin to see bubbles rising from the bottom of the yolk. Gently lift the edge of the white to find out if it's starting to brown on the bottom. If you like your egg *sunny-side up*, then it's probably done. If the top is still too runny, cover the pan with a lid for just a minute so the egg sets, then lift carefully from the pan and serve.

If you want your egg *over easy*, very, very gently lift the egg with a spatula and carefully flip it onto the other side. The big trick again is to avoid breaking the yolk. Let the egg cook for no more than 30 seconds. You may need a bit of practice until you get it right — but you will.

### Five easy ways to turn eggs into dinner

**Scrambled Eggs, Ham and Cheese Panini**
Fill a soft panini roll with scrambled eggs, sliced ham or prosciutto and cheese. Toast on both sides in a sandwich grill or frying pan, pressing to flatten.

**Egg Fried Rice**
Prepare Fried Rice with Whatever (see recipe on page 82), but use scrambled eggs instead of any meat, fish or chicken.

**Egg-Drop Ramen Noodles**
Stir a beaten egg into your favorite instant ramen noodles. Let cook, stirring, until the egg sets in ribbons, and you're done.

**Eggs in Your Salad**
Chop up a hard-boiled egg or two and toss with your green salad. Add some crumbled cooked bacon if you want and serve with fresh crusty bread.

**Just Put an Egg on It!**
Cook a flat egg (see above) and put it on top of anything you think it might be good with. Salad? Sure! Tacos? Why not? Pizza — go ahead. Grilled cheese sandwich? Bowl of noodle soup? Chili? Yes, yes and yes.

# Fast Frittata

*A frittata is like an omelet, only easier. It's like a quiche, but without a crust. Some eggs, a couple of mushrooms, three stalks of asparagus, an old onion, a withered potato — no finicky messing around, no fancy folding, and dinner is served.*

6 eggs, beaten
¼ cup (60 ml) olive oil or vegetable oil
1 medium onion, chopped
1½ cups (375 ml) raw or cooked vegetables, sliced or diced (raw mushrooms,
    zucchini, sweet peppers, spinach, asparagus; cooked potatoes, green beans,
    corn, carrots, broccoli — use your imagination and whatever is in the fridge)
¼ cup (60 ml) grated Parmesan cheese, divided
2 tbsp. (30 ml) butter or additional oil
½ tsp. (2 ml) salt
¼ tsp. (1 ml) black pepper

Crack the eggs into a large bowl and whisk them until evenly yellow. Set aside.

Heat the oil in a 10-inch (25 cm) skillet (non-stick if you have one) over medium heat. Add the chopped onion and cook, stirring, for about 5 minutes, or until the onion is softened. Toss in whatever raw vegetables you're using and cook for a few minutes, until they're softened. Now add any cooked vegetables and sauté for 1 or 2 minutes, just to heat through and give them a chance to become friends.

Add vegetable mixture to the beaten eggs in the bowl, along with *half* of the Parmesan cheese, and the salt and pepper. In the same skillet in which you cooked the vegetables, heat the butter or additional oil over medium heat. When the pan is hot, pour in the egg–vegetable mixture and spread it around evenly. Reduce the heat to low and let the egg mixture cook gently for 15 to 20 minutes, just until the eggs are set around the edges but still a little wobbly in the middle. Remove from heat.

Preheat the broiler element in your oven and place the top oven rack as close to the element as possible.

Sprinkle the remaining Parmesan cheese over the top of the frittata, place it under the preheated broiler and broil for 1 to 2 minutes, just until the top is set and lightly browned.

Remove the skillet from the oven, loosen the edges of the frittata with a knife and slide it out onto a plate. Or, if it simply refuses to exit the pan, serve it directly from the skillet and pretend that was your plan all along.

Cut into wedges and serve hot, or let cool and serve at room temperature.

## Bacon, of course!

If you're having eggs, bacon is inevitable, isn't it? Here are three ways to cook an egg's best friend.

### In a skillet

Lay as many slices into a cold skillet as will fit without overlapping (much). Adjust the burner to medium heat and cook for 6 to 8 minutes, flipping and rearranging the slices often, until they're done the way you like — crisp or still a bit chewy. Drain the slices on a paper towel–lined plate for a minute before serving.

### In the oven

Preheat the oven to 400°F (200°C). Line a rimmed cookie sheet with foil. Lay all the bacon slices in the pan without overlapping and place the pan in the preheated oven. Bacon should be cooked to crisp perfection in 15 to 20 minutes, but check after 10 minutes to see how it's doing. Remove slices to a paper towel–lined plate to drain for a minute before serving.

### In the microwave

Arrange up to 8 slices of bacon on a microwave-safe baking dish — don't overlap them. Cover with a single layer of paper towel. Microwave on high power for 45 seconds to 1 minute per strip of bacon. Rearrange the strips halfway through the cooking time so they cook evenly.

# Middle Eastern Shakshuka

serves 2

*Is it a dance? A disease? A small furry animal? None of the above. Shakshuka is a deliciously saucy concoction of eggs poached in a tasty tomato sauce. Excellent for brunch, perfect for dinner, good enough for company.*

2 tbsp. (30 ml) olive oil or vegetable oil
1 medium onion, chopped
1 jalapeño pepper, chopped (optional, if you want a little heat)
2 cloves garlic, minced or pressed
2 tsp. (10 ml) paprika
½ tsp. (2 ml) ground cumin
2 cups (500 ml) diced tomatoes, fresh or canned
⅓ cup (75 ml) water
½ tsp. (2 ml) salt
¼ tsp. (1 ml) black pepper
4 eggs
½ cup (125 ml) crumbled feta cheese
¼ cup (60 ml) chopped fresh parsley or cilantro

Heat the oil in a 10-inch (25 cm) skillet over medium heat. Add the onions and jalapeño pepper (if you're using it), and cook, stirring, for about 5 minutes, or until softened. Add the garlic, paprika and cumin, and continue cooking for about 2 minutes. Stir in the tomatoes, water, salt and pepper, and cook, stirring often, until the sauce begins to thicken — about 10 minutes.

Crack one of the eggs into a small bowl — be careful not to break the yolk. With a spoon, make an indentation in the simmering sauce — this doesn't have to be perfect — and gently drop the egg into the little nest. Repeat with the remaining eggs. Try to keep them as far apart from one another in the pan as possible so that they don't fuse. Cover the pan with a lid and cook for 5 or 6 minutes, basting the eggs once or twice with the sauce, until they're set but the yolks are still runny.

Sprinkle the feta cheese and cilantro or parsley over the top of the whole mess, cover the pan for no more than 1 minute and serve.

This goes well with warm pita bread or a crusty baguette to soak up all that delicious sauce.

# Quickie Quiche

serves 4–6

*Fancy French cousin to the Italian frittata, a quiche is really just another way to turn a humble mess of odds and ends into a delicious meal. If you use a frozen, ready-to-bake pastry shell, you can throw a quiche together in about 15 minutes. If you want to make your own pastry (see page 186) it'll take a little longer.*

2 tbsp. (30 ml) olive oil or vegetable oil

1 medium onion, chopped

1½ cups (375 ml) prepared vegetables or other filling ingredients (see sidebar)

2 cups (500 ml) shredded Swiss or cheddar cheese

3 eggs

1 cup (250 ml) milk or plain yogurt

½ tsp. (2 ml) salt

¼ tsp. (1 ml) black pepper

9-inch (23 cm) unbaked pastry crust, store-bought or homemade

## Mix-and-match quiche ideas

Pick one, pick two, pick three — it's your quiche and you get to decide what goes in it!

- sliced cooked or raw mushrooms
- sliced cooked or raw zucchini
- crumbled cooked bacon
- chopped cooked spinach or raw baby spinach leaves
- chopped cooked green beans
- diced cooked ham
- cooked or raw broccoli florets
- diced cooked chicken
- chopped cooked or raw asparagus
- shredded carrots
- crumbled cooked sausage meat
- sliced or chopped fresh tomatoes

Preheat the oven to 375°F (190°C).

Heat the oil in a medium skillet over medium heat. Add the onion and cook, stirring, for 6 to 8 minutes, until softened. Stir in whatever raw vegetables you're using and cook for a few minutes, until just tender. Now add any cooked filling ingredients and heat briefly, stirring just until combined with the onion mixture. Let cool for a minute.

Spread the filling mixture over the bottom of the pastry crust. Sprinkle with the shredded cheese.

In a bowl, beat together the eggs and the milk or yogurt. Add the salt and pepper, and pour this mixture over the cheese in the pastry crust.

Place the quiche in the preheated oven and bake for 35 to 40 minutes, until puffed slightly in the middle and golden on top. If you poke a knife into the middle of the quiche, it should come out clean, with no egg clinging to it. Let cool for a minute or two before serving.

# Oatmeal from Scratch

*You don't ever have to buy expensive packets of instant oatmeal. Rolled oats cook quickly enough and don't contain any artificial flavor or sugar. Add berries or a banana and sweeten it to your taste — so much better! Here's how to make it either on the stovetop or in the microwave.*

1 cup (250 ml) cold water
½ cup (125 ml) quick-cooking rolled oats (not instant)

## To cook on the stovetop

Combine the water and the oats in a small saucepan and bring to a boil over medium heat. Cook, stirring, for about 5 minutes, or until as thick as you like it.

## To cook in the microwave

Mix the water and oats in a large microwave-safe bowl. Microwave on high power for 2 minutes, stir, then microwave for another 1 or 2 minutes, stirring every 30 seconds, until thickened to your taste.

Either way, serve your homemade oatmeal drizzled with honey, sprinkled with brown sugar and cinnamon, swimming in maple syrup, glopped with strawberry jam or drowned in milk.

That's it. Done. One gooey, delicious serving.

## Fruit-it-up!

Add any of these to your oatmeal before cooking:
- ½ cup (125 ml) fresh or frozen berries
- ½ cup (125 ml) chopped apple, pear or peach
- ½ banana, peeled and sliced
- ¼ cup (60 ml) raisins or dried cranberries
- ¼ cup (60 ml) chopped walnuts or pecans

# Cheese and Bread Strata

serves 6–8

*Assemble this in the evening, slide it into the oven the next morning and then go set the table or walk the dog. In about an hour you will have magically created the best brunch dish ever, without lifting a finger. Except, of course, to turn on the oven. You'll look like a genius. Just smile and say you're welcome.*

16 to 20 slices bread, any kind — fresh or stale
4 cups (1 liter) shredded cheese, any kind
  (a mixture is fine)
4 green onions, chopped
5 eggs, beaten
3 cups (750 ml) milk
1 tbsp. (15 ml) prepared mustard
  (Dijon, if you have it)
1 tsp. (5 ml) salt
¼ tsp. (1 ml) cayenne pepper
1 or 2 medium tomatoes, sliced
⅓ cup (75 ml) grated Parmesan cheese

## Optional additions (choose one or more)

- browned sausage meat
- raw baby spinach leaves
- sautéed hot or sweet peppers
- sautéed mushrooms
- chopped cooked bacon
- sautéed zucchini slices

Grease a 9 x 13-inch (23 x 33 cm) rectangular baking dish.

Line the prepared baking dish with a layer of bread slices. (You may need to cut them up a bit so they cover the bottom, jigsaw puzzle–style. Don't obsess over this — just do the best you can.) Sprinkle the bread with 1/3 of the cheese and 1/3 of the green onions. If you're using any of the optional ingredients (see above), add them along with the green onions in each layer. Repeat two more times: bread, cheese, onions, bread, cheese, onions — making a total of 3 layers of each, ending with green onions.

In a bowl, beat the eggs with the milk, mustard, salt and cayenne. Pour milk mixture over the layers in the baking dish, cover the whole thing with foil or plastic wrap and refrigerate overnight. Or longer. Even a couple of days in the fridge is okay.

When you're ready to bake, remove strata from the refrigerator and preheat the oven to 350°F (180°C).

Unwrap the baking dish, arrange the tomato slices artistically on top and sprinkle with Parmesan cheese. Place in the oven and bake for 50 to 60 minutes, or until slightly puffed in the middle and lightly browned on top. If you poke a knife into the center of the strata, it should come out clean.

# French Toast for Two

*It's easy to imagine how French toast was invented, isn't it? Leftover bread, an egg, a little milk. It just happened. Feel free to halve, double or triple this recipe depending on whether you're dining solo or feeding a crowd.*

2 eggs
¼ cup (60 ml) milk
4 slices bread, any kind, stale or fresh
1 tbsp. (15 ml) vegetable oil
Cinnamon for sprinkling, if desired

In a flattish bowl, beat together the egg with the milk. Dip the bread slices into this mixture, turning to coat both sides.

Pour the oil into a small frying pan and place over medium heat. Lay the bread slices in the pan, sprinkle lightly with cinnamon (if you like) and cook until golden brown on one side. Flip over and cook the other side until golden brown, then remove to a plate.

Serve immediately with maple syrup, jam, cinnamon sugar, sliced strawberries or anything else that makes you happy.

## Making soured milk — and why you'd ever want to do such a thing

Sometimes you may come across a recipe that calls for sour milk. In the olden days before milk was routinely pasteurized, milk that went sour was used as an ingredient in cooking and baking to help things like muffins and pancakes rise. Pasteurized milk doesn't sour quite the same way, so we have to cheat a little. Not a problem.

**Cheat 1:** Measure 1 tbsp. (15 ml) vinegar or lemon juice into a measuring cup. Fill the cup to the 1 cup (250 ml) level with milk and stir to mix. Let sit for about 5 minutes before using. The milk will go all icky and lumpy — exactly what you want. Congratulations! You have now made 1 cup (250 ml) soured milk that you can use in any recipe that calls for sour milk.

**Cheat 2:** Substitute the same amount of commercial buttermilk for the sour milk in any recipe that calls for it.

**Cheat 3:** Or use plain yogurt. Mix with just enough milk to make it pourable and use in any recipe that calls for sour milk or buttermilk.

# Pancakes Not from a Box

serves 3–4

*Believe it or not, it's possible to make pancakes without a mix. And it's not even hard.*

1¼ cups (300 ml) all-purpose flour
1 tbsp. (15 ml) granulated sugar
1 tbsp. (15 ml) baking powder
1 egg
1 cup (250 ml) milk
2 tbsp. (30 ml) vegetable oil
Additional oil for cooking

In a medium-size bowl, stir together the flour, sugar and baking powder. In another bowl, beat together the egg, milk and vegetable oil. Add the egg mixture to the flour mixture and stir until combined — a few lumps don't matter.

Pour a small amount of vegetable oil into a large skillet — just enough to coat the surface with a film of oil. Place the skillet over medium heat and let it heat until a drop of water sizzles when you sprinkle it in. Spoon about 1/4 cup (60 ml) of the batter into the pan, spreading it evenly. (If the batter is too thick to pour easily, stir in a little additional milk to thin it.) Allow the pancake to cook on one side until bubbles appear on the top, then flip it and let the other side cook until golden. Remove to a plate and repeat with the remaining batter, adding more oil to the frying pan as needed.

Once you get good at this, you can try cooking more than one pancake at a time in a large skillet.

Serve immediately with the usual accompaniments — and act casual when people go crazy.

Makes about fourteen 4-inch (10 cm) pancakes, 3 to 4 servings.

# Whole Wheat Blueberry Yogurt Pancakes

*Eat these pancakes and you'll feel so healthy it's scary. Loaded with good stuff —
they're a perfect way to start your day.*

1¼ cups (300 ml) whole wheat flour
1 tbsp. (15 ml) granulated sugar
1 tsp. (5 ml) baking powder
½ tsp. (2 ml) baking soda
1¼ cups (300 ml) plain yogurt, buttermilk or soured milk (see page 135)
2 tbsp. (30 ml) vegetable oil
1 egg
1 cup (250 ml) fresh or frozen blueberries
Additional oil for cooking

In a medium bowl, combine the whole wheat flour, sugar, baking powder and
baking soda. In another bowl, stir together the yogurt (or buttermilk or soured
milk), oil and egg. Add the yogurt mixture to the flour mixture and stir just until
combined. Gently fold in the blueberries. Don't overbeat this batter, because
you'll deflate the fluffiness. (If the batter is too thick to pour easily, add up to 1/2
cup/125 ml milk to thin it.)

Pour a small amount of vegetable oil into a large skillet — just enough to coat
the surface with a film of oil. Place the skillet over medium heat and let it heat
until a drop of water sizzles when you sprinkle it in. Spoon about 1/4 cup (60 ml)
of the batter into the pan, spreading it evenly. Allow the pancake to cook on
one side until bubbles appear on the top, then flip it and let the other side cook
until golden. The blueberries will leak juice as the pancakes cook — that's okay.
Remove to a plate and repeat with the remaining batter, adding more oil to the
skillet as needed.

Serve immediately, or keep them in a warm (250°F/120°C) oven until all the
pancakes are finished. Maple syrup is a must.

Makes about fourteen 4-inch (10 cm) pancakes, 3 to 4 servings.

# Crepes

*Once you get the hang of making crepes, you'll think of a million things to do with them. They make a very impressive breakfast, lunch, dinner or even dessert. See the filling suggestions below or come up with your own fabulous creations. These will make you famous.*

1 cup (250 ml) all-purpose flour
2 eggs
1¾ cups (425 ml) milk
1 tsp. (5 ml) granulated sugar (for use with sweet fillings)
½ tsp. (2 ml) salt (for use with savory fillings)
Vegetable oil for cooking

Put all the ingredients into the container of a blender and blend until smooth. Pour the batter into a bowl, cover it and refrigerate for at least 1 hour before using. This standing time is essential — it allows the batter to thicken slightly and makes it easier to work with.

Lightly coat an 8 or 9-inch (20 to 25 cm) non-stick skillet with vegetable oil and place over medium heat, until a drop of water sizzles as soon as it hits the pan.

Pour about 1/4 cup (60 ml) of the crepe batter into the pan, swirling the pan to coat the bottom evenly. If necessary, spread the batter out with a knife or spatula so that it forms a thin, even layer. This is the part that takes a bit of practice, so don't feel bad if the first few crepes turn out weird. Just quickly eat them and say nothing.

When the top of the crepe starts to look a bit dry and the

## Crepe fillings for every occasion

### Savory
- sliced mushrooms sautéed in butter, sprinkled with shredded cheese and seasoned with salt and pepper
- sweet peppers sautéed with onions and tomatoes and sprinkled with shredded cheese
- sliced cooked ham and Swiss cheese, heated in the oven until the cheese melts
- steamed broccoli, sprinkled with lemon juice, salt, pepper and shredded Swiss cheese
- cooked bacon with spinach and cheese

### Sweet
- sliced apples sautéed in butter with sugar, cinnamon and lemon juice
- fresh berries or peaches sweetened with maple syrup and served with whipped cream
- apricot or strawberry jam
- sweetened ricotta cheese and fresh strawberries

bottom is just beginning to brown (peek underneath to check), carefully flip the crepe over with a pancake turner. Cook for no more than 30 seconds — just long enough to set — then remove to a plate. (Cover and keep warm if you'll be using them right away.)

Lightly coat the pan again with oil and repeat the process until you have used up all of the batter.

Makes 10 to 12 crepes if all goes well.

# Things on the Side

Don't let your main dish get lonely. Keep it company with a little something on the side. It might be an excellent vegetable concoction or it can be a scoop of perfectly cooked rice. Here are some very tasty side dishes that will add that extra little something to your meal.

# Oven-Roasted Vegetables

*Think of this more as a suggestion than an actual recipe. Go ahead and mess with it to use whatever vegetables you happen to have in the house. Substitute chunks of butternut squash for sweet potatoes, or invite some broccoli, cauliflower or carrots to the party. Just make sure you cut everything up into similar-size pieces so they cook evenly.*

2 medium sweet potatoes, peeled
2 medium onions, peeled
1 medium sweet red pepper
½ lb. (250 ml) fresh mushrooms
1 medium zucchini
¼ cup (60 ml) olive oil or vegetable oil
2 cloves garlic, minced or pressed
½ tsp. (2 ml) salt
¼ tsp. (1 ml) black pepper
Chopped fresh parsley or basil (or both!) if you have it

Preheat the oven to 425°F (220°C). Grease a large, shallow baking pan — like a lasagna pan or rimmed cookie sheet.

Trim all the vegetables, removing stems or cores or whatever they happen to have, and cut into 1-inch (2 cm) chunks. If the mushrooms are very large, cut them in half; otherwise leave them whole. Place in a bowl and toss with the oil, garlic, salt and pepper.

Spread the vegetables out in a single layer in the prepared baking pan. Use two pans if you have to, so that the vegetables have enough room to brown properly. Bake in the preheated oven for 40 to 45 minutes, tossing occasionally, until all the vegetables are tender and well browned. Sprinkle with fresh parsley or basil before serving.

# Shake and Bake Zucchini Sticks    serves 4

*Try these with a creamy dip as an appetizer or snack, or serve them as a side dish. Addictively excellent.*

¼ cup (60 ml) vegetable oil, divided
4 medium zucchini
½ cup (125 ml) dry bread crumbs
½ cup (125 ml) grated Parmesan cheese
½ tsp. (2 ml) garlic powder
½ tsp. (2 ml) salt
¼ tsp. (1 ml) black pepper
1 egg, beaten

Preheat the oven to 425°F (220°C). Pour half of the vegetable oil onto a rimmed cookie sheet and spread it to coat the bottom evenly.

Trim the stem and blossom ends off the zucchini and cut the zucchini into sticks approximately 1/2 inch (1 cm) thick and 3 inches (8 cm) long.

In a small bowl, mix together the bread crumbs, Parmesan cheese, garlic powder, salt and pepper. Dump this mixture into a clean plastic bag.

Working with about 3 or 4 zucchini sticks at a time, first dip them into the beaten egg, then fish them out (letting the excess egg drip back into the bowl) and toss them into the bag with the bread crumb mixture. Shake to coat, then remove them from the bag and arrange on the cookie sheet. Repeat until you have used up all the zucchini sticks or crumbs or (ideally) both.

Drizzle the remaining oil over the breaded zucchini sticks, place the pan in the preheated oven and bake for 15 to 20 minutes, turning them over about halfway through the baking time. They should be nicely browned and sizzling.

# An incomplete guide to vegetable cookery

So there it sits. Broccoli. Or spinach. Or whatever it is. You've eaten it cooked, but how do you get there? This thing is raw! Relax — it's just a harmless vegetable. You're bigger and smarter and you have a knife. Here are some guidelines to help you grapple with the most common vegetables you're likely to encounter.

**Asparagus** Sorry — did that scare you? No really, asparagus is easy. Rinse and trim off the cut end of each spear. Cut in pieces or leave whole.
**To cook:** Steam (see broccoli) until bright green and not a moment longer. Or roast (see cauliflower) for 15 to 20 minutes, until beginning to brown. Either way — delicious.

**Broccoli** Wash well and cut the bottom off each stem. Cut the stem into chunks and the top into individual florets.
**To cook:** Steam in a steamer basket over boiling water or boil in water until the broccoli becomes bright green. At this point the broccoli is perfect — tender but still crisp. Overcooked broccoli is mushy and swampy green, and loses all its charm, so don't do that.

**Carrots** Scrub well and peel if you want. Cut into slices, cubes or sticks.
**To cook:** Steam in a steamer basket over boiling water, or simmer in enough water to cover, or sauté in oil or butter until tender but not mushy.

**Cauliflower** Trim off any leaves and cut the head of cauliflower into individual florets. Rinse well.
**To cook:** Yes, you can steam or boil (see broccoli), but there is a better way. Drizzle the prepared cauliflower with olive oil, salt and pepper, and toss until all the pieces are lightly coated. Dump onto a rimmed cookie sheet and spread the pieces out in a single layer. Roast at 425°F (220°C) for 30 to 40 minutes, stirring once or twice, until lightly browned. Shockingly good.

**Corn** On the cob or off — it's all good.
**To cook:** For corn *on* the cob, peel off the husk, pull off the hairy bits and either steam the cob in a steamer basket over boiling water or boil in a large pot of salted water for at least 5 minutes but no longer than 10. The kernels should be tender but still have some crunch when you take a bite. You can also cut the kernels off the cob and sauté them alone or with other vegetables in butter or oil. Kernels of freshly cooked corn are a great addition to soups and salads.

**Mushrooms** Rinse whole mushrooms and drain well or dry on paper towel. Trim stems and either leave whole or slice them or cut into chunks.
**To cook:** Sauté in butter or olive oil until softened. They get along well with

onions and garlic. Large mushrooms (portobello) can be cut into large chunks, tossed with oil and roasted (see cauliflower).

**Spinach** Pick over and remove any wilted leaves or non-spinach bits. Rinse well.

**To cook:** Place rinsed spinach in a large pot with just the water that clings to the leaves after rinsing. Cover with a lid and cook over medium-high heat until wilted. Drain excess liquid before serving. You can also stir-fry spinach or sauté in butter or oil.

**String Beans — Green, Yellow, Purple, Whatever** Wash and snap off the stem end. Cut into pieces or leave whole.

**To cook:** Steam in a steamer basket over boiling water or simmer in water until tender but still a little crisp and still brightly colored.

**Winter Squash — Butternut, Acorn, Hubbard, Delicata, Butter-cup (and more)** Most winter squash has a thick skin and central cavity that contains the seeds. So peel if you want, using a vegetable peeler, and cut in half. Scoop out the seeds and cut into cubes or pieces. If you plan to bake the squash in its skin, just cut in half and scoop out the seeds.

**To cook:** You can steam or boil squash cubes if you want (see carrots). Or you can toss the squash cubes with olive oil or vegetable oil, season with salt and pepper, and roast on a cookie sheet (see cauliflower). Or you can bake halved or quartered squash in the skin, cut-side down on a cookie sheet at 400°F (200°C) for 30 to 45 minutes. Turn squash over halfway through the baking time to allow excess water to evaporate.

**Zucchini** Wash and slice crosswise into 1/4-inch (.5 cm) pieces. Or cut into 1/2-inch (1 cm) cubes. Your choice.

**To cook:** Zucchini is best sautéed with a little olive oil or vegetable oil over medium-high heat. It plays well with onions, peppers and garlic.

## Four sweet ways with sweet potatoes

- Bake them whole like regular potatoes, until soft.
- Cut them into chunks, toss with olive oil, garlic, salt and pepper, and roast on a rimmed cookie sheet at 425°F (220°C) until tender and browned.
- Bake, peel, then mash with maple syrup and butter.
- Peel, cube and steam until just tender. Let cool and toss with Basic Vinaigrette Dressing (see recipe on page 48) for a sweet potato salad.

# How to cook rice

You don't ever need to use instant rice. The real thing tastes better, is cheaper and doesn't take much time to cook, anyway. The ratio of rice to liquid can vary depending on the type of rice you have. If your rice turns out too mushy, use less liquid next time. If it's not quite cooked, add a bit more liquid.

**White Rice**  Simple, basic and it goes with anything.
1 cup (250 ml) white rice (see page 151 for different varieties)
1½ cups (375 ml) water

Measure the water into a saucepan with a tight-fitting lid. Bring it to a boil over high heat. Add the rice to the boiling water and give it a stir. Lower the heat to the barest simmer and cover with the lid. Let cook for 15 minutes without peeking.

After 15 minutes, lift the lid and have a look. The water should be completely absorbed and the surface of the rice should look as if there are holes all over it. Don't stir, but taste a grain or two to see if the rice is done. If it's not quite cooked, replace the lid and give it another 5 minutes, then test again. When the rice is cooked, remove the pan from the heat and let stand, covered, for about 5 minutes, then fluff with a fork and serve.

Makes about 2 1/2 cups (625 ml) plain white rice.

**Brown Rice**  Slightly chewy, nutty, delicious. Brown rice takes a little longer to cook than white, but it's really nutritious and the flavor goes especially well with beans and other hearty things.
1 cup (250 ml) brown rice
2½ cups (625 ml) water

Measure the water into a saucepan with a tight-fitting lid. Bring it to a boil over high heat. Add the rice to the boiling water and give it a stir. Lower the heat to the barest simmer and cover with the lid. Let cook for 35 minutes without peeking.

After 35 minutes, lift the lid and have a look. The water should be completely absorbed and the surface of the rice should look as if there are holes all over it. Don't stir, but taste a grain or two to see if the rice is tender. If it's not quite cooked, replace the lid and give it another 5 or 10 minutes, then taste again. When the rice is cooked, remove the pan from the heat and let stand, covered, for about 5 minutes, then fluff with a fork and serve.

Makes 3 1/2 cups (875 ml) plain brown rice.

# Crazy Easy Risotto

*Maybe you've eaten risotto in a restaurant or at someone's home. This Italian rice dish is often considered time-consuming to make (it isn't) and finicky (not at all). Try this simplified recipe and you may just impress your Italian grandmother. If you have one, that is.*

2 tbsp. (30 ml) olive oil or vegetable oil
1 tbsp. (15 ml) butter
1 medium onion, chopped
2 cups (500 ml) prepared vegetables (see sidebar opposite for ideas)
1½ cups (375 ml) Arborio rice (yes, you should use this kind)
4 cups (1 liter) chicken or vegetable broth (prepared broth or made from bouillon cubes or powder)
¼ cup (60 ml) grated Parmesan cheese (plus more to sprinkle at the table)
½ tsp. (2 ml) salt
¼ tsp. (1 ml) black pepper

In a medium saucepan with a tight-fitting lid, combine the oil and butter, and place over medium heat. Add the onion and cook, stirring often, for 5 to 7 minutes, or until softened and beginning to turn golden.

If you're using *mushrooms*, add them now. Cook, stirring, until the mushrooms have softened and released their juices and the liquid has almost entirely evaporated — 5 to 7 minutes.

Add the rice and stir for a couple of minutes, then add all the broth. If you're using *any other vegetable except for mushrooms*, add it now along with the broth. Bring to a boil, stirring to prevent the rice from sticking to the bottom of the pot. As soon as it reaches a boil, reduce the heat to low, cover the pot with the lid and cook — without stirring or looking or any kind of fussing whatsoever — for 15 minutes.

After 15 minutes, remove the lid, stir in the Parmesan cheese, salt and pepper. The risotto should be creamy but not runny. If it's too dry, you can add a bit of water or broth to loosen it up. The risotto will thicken as it cools.

Serve immediately with additional Parmesan for sprinkling at the table.

### Risotto possibilities
- thinly sliced fresh mushrooms
- fresh asparagus, cut into ½-inch (1 cm) pieces
- broccoli florets
- fresh or frozen peas
- fresh spinach, chopped (add only in the last 10 minutes of cooking time)
- butternut squash, peeled and cut into ½-inch (1 cm) cubes
- zucchini, cut into ½-inch (1 cm) cubes

# Cumin-Flavored Yellow Rice

serves 2–3

*Fantastic with Indian curries, excellent with chili, perfect with beans or spicy stews. Also very pretty.*

1 tbsp. (15 ml) olive oil or vegetable oil
1 medium onion, chopped
1 tsp. (5 ml) whole cumin seeds
½ tsp. (2 ml) turmeric
½ tsp. (2 ml) salt
2 cups (500 ml) water
1 cup (250 ml) white rice (basmati, if you have it)

Heat the oil in a medium saucepan over medium-low heat. Add the onion and cook, stirring often, for 5 to 7 minutes, until softened and beginning to turn golden.

Add the cumin seeds, turmeric and salt, and continue cooking for 1 or 2 minutes, stirring constantly.

Add the water and rice, increase the heat to medium and bring to a boil. As soon as the mixture boils, reduce the heat to low, cover the pot and let cook for about 15 minutes, until all the liquid has been absorbed and the rice is tender.

## Fancy-it-up easy!

**Lemony Rice**
To the recipe for basic rice, add one tbsp. (15 ml) butter, ½ tsp. (5 ml) salt, and the juice and zest of one whole lemon. Cook as for plain rice. Deliciously lemony — goes well with chicken and fish.

**Sort of Pilaf**
Toss ½ cup (125 ml) frozen corn or peas into basic rice recipe and use chicken or vegetable broth (any prepared broth or from bouillon cube or powder) as the cooking liquid.

**Kinda Mexican**
Sauté a chopped onion in oil along with 1 tsp. (5 ml) Mexican chili powder and ½ tsp. (2 ml) salt. Add to the basic rice recipe and use tomato juice as the cooking liquid.

**Coconut Rice**
Instead of water in the basic rice recipe, use canned coconut milk as the cooking liquid. Add ½ tsp. (2 ml) salt and cook as for plain rice. Perfect with beans and spicy Asian dishes.

# Other grainy things for your repertoire

Once in a while a person needs something else. Not rice, but sort of like rice. Something to soak up the sauce or serve with the stew. Here are some nifty alternatives for when you're feeling a little wild and crazy.

**Quinoa** Pronounced keen-wah, this little grain was a favorite of the Incas of Peru. It's extremely nutritious, really tasty and very easy to cook. You can serve it as a side dish — it's like rice, only more fun. (Look closely at the cooked grains — they're adorable!)

1 cup (250 ml) quinoa
1½ cups (375 ml) water

Before cooking quinoa, you'll need to rinse the grains well to remove a natural coating that may remain on them. Measure the quinoa into a strainer (with very small holes) and run water over it, stirring it with your fingers to make sure it's well rinsed. Let it drain while you bring the water to a boil. (Some packaged quinoa is prerinsed, making this step unnecessary — it will say so on the package. If you're not sure, just rinse before using.)

Measure the water into a saucepan with a tight-fitting lid. Bring water to a boil over high heat. Add the rinsed quinoa and give it a stir. When the water returns to a boil, turn the heat down to low, cover the pot and let cook, undisturbed, for 15 minutes. Turn off the heat and let the quinoa sit for another 5 minutes before serving. Fluff and serve.

Makes 2 1/2 cups (625 ml) cooked quinoa.

**Couscous** Technically, couscous is a tiny form of pasta. It's made from wheat and comes in different varieties — regular, whole wheat, vegetable flavored. It cooks in minutes and goes with just about anything. What's not to like?

1 cup (250 ml) water or broth (any kind)
1 tbsp. (15 ml) olive oil, vegetable oil or butter
1 cup (250 ml) couscous
½ tsp. (2 ml) salt

In a medium saucepan, combine the liquid with the oil or butter and bring to a boil over high heat. Stir in the dry couscous and salt, cover with a lid and turn off the heat. Let stand for 5 to 10 minutes. The grains will absorb all the liquid and become tender. Fluff with a fork and serve.

No, seriously — that's it.

Makes about 2 cups (500 ml) couscous.

## Couscous gone wild!

**Herbed Lemon Couscous:** Stir in 1 tbsp. (15 ml) chopped fresh parsley and 1 tbsp. (15 ml) lemon juice when you add the couscous to the liquid.

**Rock the Casbah Couscous:** Stir in 2 tbsp. (30 ml) raisins, 1/4 tsp. (1 ml) cinnamon, 1/4 tsp. (1 ml) turmeric and 1/4 tsp. (1 ml) ground cumin when you add the couscous to the liquid.

**Tomato Basil Couscous:** Add 2 chopped sun-dried tomatoes, 2 chopped green onions and 1 tbsp. (15 ml) chopped fresh basil when you stir the couscous into the liquid.

**Barley** You've seen it floating around in soup, but it's also a delicious addition to a mixed-grain pilaf or a salad. Pearl barley cooks more quickly than pot (or hulled) barley, but either one can be used.

1 cup (250 ml) barley
3 cups (750 ml) water

Rinse the barley in a strainer under cold running water to remove excess starch. In a medium saucepan with a tight-fitting lid, combine the barley and water, and bring to a boil over high heat. Reduce the heat to low, cover the pan and cook the grain until all the water has been absorbed and the barley is tender — 35 to 45 minutes. When the barley is cooked, remove the pan from the heat and let stand, covered, for 5 minutes. Fluff with a fork and serve immediately, or let cool and use in a salad or other dish.

Makes about 4 cups (1 liter).

**Bulgur Wheat** Bulgur is a form of whole wheat that has been partially cooked, then dehydrated and cracked into small granules. Because it's pre-cooked, bulgur only needs to be soaked in boiling water before using. It makes a mean tabbouleh salad (see page 46) but can also be served as a side dish in place of rice or couscous.

1 cup (250 ml) bulgur wheat
2 cups (500 ml) boiling water or broth (any kind)

Put the bulgur in a bowl or saucepan. Add the boiling water or broth, stir, then cover the bowl and let stand until the water has been absorbed, about 5 to 10 minutes. The bulgur will be chewy but tender and can be used in a salad or seasoned to taste and served as a side dish.

Makes about 3 cups (750 ml).

# Around the world with rice

Rice comes in so many different varieties — it can be confusing. Each type has its own characteristics and is best used in certain dishes. Here are just a few of the most common varieties of rice that you may want to try.

### Arborio rice

Italian short grain rice, essential for risotto and really excellent for rice pudding.

### Basmati rice

This aromatic rice from India comes in both white and brown varieties. It has a wonderfully nutty flavor and very fluffy, long grains. Best for pilaf and to go with curries.

### Brown rice

This is what rice was before they sanded the outsides off. Tasty, chewy, full of nutrients and fiber and other good stuff. Can be used instead of white rice in many recipes but requires a longer cooking time.

### Converted (or parboiled) rice

This is white rice that has been steamed before milling. The grains stay separate when cooked and the rice retains more vitamins than regular white rice does. Excellent to use in casseroles or in any dish that will have to sit for a while after cooking but before serving.

### Instant rice

Rice that has been completely cooked, then dehydrated. Recommended for mountain climbing and other desperate survival situations.

### Jasmine rice

A fragrant, medium-grain rice. Widely used in Thai and other Asian cooking. This is a good all-purpose white rice to keep on hand — can be used in any recipe that calls for white rice.

### Long grain white rice

All-purpose rice that cooks up fluffy and light. Easily available everywhere. Can be used in most recipes that call for white rice.

### Wild rice

Technically, this is not rice at all, but since it sort of looks like it, we're going to lump it together with the rest. Very tasty and chewy — it's often a wild product harvested from northern lakes. Since it's quite expensive, you may want to use it mixed with another type of rice, like brown or white basmati.

# Refried Beans

*Canned refried beans can be salty and greasy, and they may contain ingredients you might prefer to avoid. Make your own — it's easy, cheap and you'll know exactly what went into them.*

2 tbsp. (30 ml) olive oil or vegetable oil
½ medium onion, finely chopped
1 clove garlic, minced or pressed
1 can (19 oz./540 ml) kidney, pinto or black beans
½ tsp. (2 ml) salt, if needed

In a medium skillet, heat the oil over medium heat. Add the onion and garlic, and sauté, stirring occasionally, for about 5 minutes, or until softened. Add the canned beans, including all the liquid from the can, to the skillet and cook, mashing with a wooden spoon or a potato masher, until the mixture is fairly thick and about half mashed. You can add a bit more liquid (water or broth) if you think the beans are getting too dry. Taste, and add salt if needed (you may not need any — the canned beans already contain salt).

Makes about 2 cups (500 ml) refried beans to use in whatever way your little heart desires (see below for ideas).

## What to do with refried beans
- Roll into a warm flour tortilla with some cheese and salsa for an easy burrito.
- Make 7 Layer Taco Dip (page 21).
- Dollop over crisp tortilla chips along with some shredded cheese and salsa and bake until gooey for deluxe nachos.
- Scramble some eggs with onions and peppers and serve with refried beans and tortillas for a delicious Mexican breakfast.

# Lumpy Mashed Potatoes serves 4

*You'll definitely want this with your meat loaf (see recipe on page 63).*

6 medium potatoes, peeled and cubed
½ cup (125 ml) milk
¼ cup (60 ml) butter
½ tsp. (2 ml) salt

First, you'll have to cook the potatoes. You can steam them or boil them. To steam, place your cubed potatoes in a steamer basket in a medium or large saucepan with 1/2 to 1 inch (1 to 2 cm) of water in the bottom. Cover, and cook over medium-high heat until the potatoes are completely tender when you poke a fork into them (the fork will go in with no resistance at all). To boil the potatoes, place them in a medium or large saucepan with just enough water to cover them completely. Cover the pot, bring to a boil over medium-high heat and cook until tender (see fork test above).

While the potatoes are cooking, combine the milk and butter in a microwave-safe bowl or measuring cup and microwave on high power for 1 to 1 1/2 minutes. The milk should be hot and the butter melted. (If you don't have a microwave, heat the milk and butter together on the stove over medium heat — the milk shouldn't boil.)

When the potatoes are done, drain off all the water but leave the potatoes in the pot. Add the hot milk mixture and the salt, and mash with a potato masher or fork until the potatoes are light and fluffy but just lumpy enough to prove you made them from scratch. (Never use a food processor or mixer to mash potatoes, because the potatoes can easily become gluey — and you definitely don't want gluey.)

Serve immediately, or cover the dish and keep in a warm oven until you are ready to eat.

# Scalloped Potatoes                    serves 6–8

*Here's a side dish that's just about substantial enough to be a main course. The baking time is longish, so plan for this.*

2 tbsp. (30 ml) all-purpose flour
1 tsp. (5 ml) salt
¼ tsp. (1 ml) black pepper
6 to 8 medium potatoes, peeled and sliced very thin (8 cups/2 liters when sliced)
1½ cups (375 ml) grated cheddar or Swiss cheese
2 tbsp. (30 ml) butter
2½ cups (625 ml) milk

Preheat the oven to 375°F (190°C). Grease a 9 x 13-inch (23 x 33 cm) baking dish.

In a small bowl, mix together the flour, salt and pepper.

Arrange about 1/3 of the potato slices over the bottom of the prepared baking dish. Sprinkle evenly with about half of the flour mixture and cover with half of the grated cheese. Repeat with another 1/3 of the potatoes and all the remaining flour mixture and cheese. Finally, cover with the remaining potato slices, dot the top with butter and pour the milk over everything. Cover the baking dish with foil, place in the preheated oven and bake for 45 minutes. Remove the foil and continue baking for another 45 to 50 minutes, or until the top is browned and the potatoes are completely tender when you poke a knife into the middle of the dish.

# Oven-Fried Potato Wedges serves 2–4

*There are times when crunchy hot potatoes are just the thing. These are delicious, addictive and a zillion times better than frozen French fries.*

6 medium potatoes, washed and cut lengthwise into wedges
   (peel them if you feel you must)
¼ cup (60 ml) olive oil or vegetable oil
1 tbsp. (15 ml) lemon juice
½ tsp. (2 ml) salt
¼ tsp. (1 ml) black pepper

Preheat the oven to 450°F (230°C). Grease a 9 x 13-inch (23 x 33 cm) baking dish.

In a large bowl, toss the potatoes with the oil, lemon juice, salt and pepper to coat them evenly. Transfer to the prepared baking dish and spread the potato wedges out so that they're in a single layer.

Place in the preheated oven and bake for at least 45 minutes, stirring them from time to time, until they're crisp and golden on all sides and perfectly tender inside.

Serve immediately with the usual French fry accompaniments.

Now, isn't that better than anything?

Makes as many as 4 servings as a side dish, but only a measly 2 servings as a stand-alone snack.

## Go crazy

Don't be afraid to try sprinkling the potatoes with seasoned salt, cayenne pepper, paprika, fresh garlic or garlic powder or crumbled herbs. Add this stuff with the salt and pepper before the pan goes into the oven.

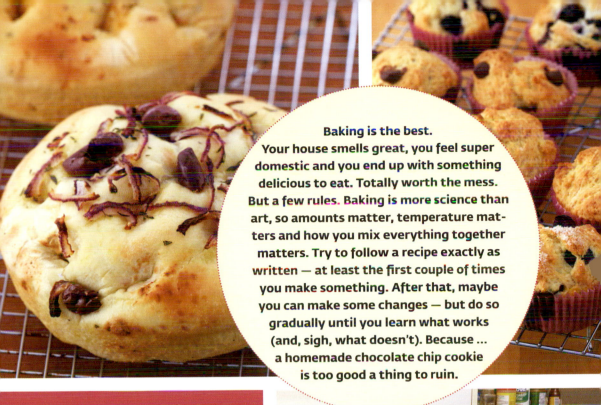

Baking is the best.
Your house smells great, you feel super domestic and you end up with something delicious to eat. Totally worth the mess. But a few rules. Baking is more science than art, so amounts matter, temperature matters and how you mix everything together matters. Try to follow a recipe exactly as written — at least the first couple of times you make something. After that, maybe you can make some changes — but do so gradually until you learn what works (and, sigh, what doesn't). Because ... a homemade chocolate chip cookie is too good a thing to ruin.

# Baking Up a Storm

# Basic Muffins
# (and not-so-basic variations)

*Even a mediocre homemade muffin, freshly baked and still warm from the oven, is so much better than anything you can buy. Try not to eat the whole batch yourself — be nice and share.*

1½ cups (375 ml) all-purpose flour
¼ cup (60 ml) granulated sugar
2½ tsp. (12 ml) baking powder
1 egg
1 cup (250 ml) milk
⅓ cup (75 ml) vegetable oil or melted butter
1 tsp. (5 ml) vanilla extract

Preheat the oven to 400°F (200°C). Grease a 12-cup muffin pan or line with paper muffin liners.

Measure the flour, sugar and baking powder into a medium bowl. In a small bowl, whisk together the egg, milk, oil or butter and vanilla. Add the egg mixture to the flour mixture all at once and stir just until the flour is evenly moistened (don't overmix — a few lumps are okay).

If you're using any of the optional ingredients (see opposite), gently stir them into the batter.

Spoon batter into the prepared muffin pan, filling the cups to within 1/4 inch (.5 cm) of the top. You'll probably have enough batter for 10 muffins — just remove the paper liners from the empty cups. Bake in the preheated oven for 20 to 25 minutes, or until a toothpick poked into the middle of a muffin comes out clean.

Makes about 10 muffins.

# Beautiful Bran Muffins

*Use natural, unprocessed bran to make these muffins, not bran flakes or bran cereal. Bran is dirt cheap and a bag of it will make a million muffins. And if you happen to plant a garden, you can sprinkle dry bran around your plants to deter slugs. Because … you just never know.*

¾ cup (175 ml) light brown sugar
½ cup (125 ml) vegetable oil
1 egg
1½ cups (375 ml) natural bran (not cereal or flakes)
1 cup (350 ml) all-purpose flour
1 tsp. (5 ml) baking soda
1 cup (250 ml) buttermilk, yogurt or soured milk (see page 135)
½ cup (125 ml) raisins or dried cranberries (optional)

Preheat the oven to 375°F (190°C). Grease a 12-cup muffin pan or line with paper muffin liners.

In a large bowl, whisk together the brown sugar, oil and egg until smooth. In another bowl, combine the bran, flour and baking soda. Add the flour mixture to the egg mixture in 2 or 3 portions, alternating with the buttermilk, yogurt or soured milk, stirring just until everything is evenly moistened. Quickly stir in the raisins or cranberries if you're using them, just until they're mixed into the batter.

Spoon batter into the prepared muffin pan, filling the cups to within 1/4 inch (.5 cm) of the top. You'll probably have enough batter for 10 muffins — just remove the paper liners from the empty cups. Bake in the preheated oven for 20 to 25 minutes, or until a toothpick poked into the middle of a muffin comes out clean.

Makes about 10 muffins.

# Corn Bread

*Is there anything that goes better with a bowl of chili than fresh corn bread? We think not.*

1½ cups (375 ml) all-purpose flour
1 cup (250 ml) yellow cornmeal
¼ cup (60 ml) granulated sugar
2 tbsp. (30 ml) baking powder
½ tsp. (2 ml) salt
¼ cup (60 ml) vegetable oil
1 egg
1⅓ cups (325 ml) milk

Preheat the oven to 350°F (180°C). Grease an 8 or 9-inch (20 or 23 cm) square baking pan.

In a large bowl, stir together the flour, cornmeal, sugar, baking powder and salt. In another bowl, whisk together the oil, egg and milk. Pour the milk mixture into the flour mixture and stir until just combined. A few lumps are okay, so don't overbeat the batter.

Pour batter into the prepared baking pan, spreading so that the top is even. Bake in the preheated oven for 15 to 20 minutes, or until lightly browned on top and a toothpick poked into the middle comes out clean.

Let cool for just a couple of minutes before cutting into squares.

Makes 9 to 12 squares of corn bread.

## Corn bread variations

Switch up your corn bread with a little something extra. Add any of the following ingredients when you combine the wet and dry mixtures:

½ cup (125 ml) dried cranberries
1 cup (250 ml) corn kernels (frozen, canned or cut from a cooked cob)
1 cup (250 ml) shredded sharp cheddar cheese
1 or 2 chopped fresh jalapeño peppers
¼ cup (60 ml) crumbled, crisply cooked bacon

# Italian Everything Dough

*Yes, it's a yeast dough. But don't be scared — it's easy and fun. You can use this dough to make your own homemade pizza (see pages 110 to 113) or the most delicious focaccia you've ever tasted (see page 161).*

3½ cups (825 ml) all-purpose flour, divided (approximately)
1 envelope quick-rise instant yeast (2¼ tsp./11 ml) granules
1 tsp. (5 ml) salt
1 cup (250 ml) hot tap water
2 tbsp. (30 ml) olive oil or vegetable oil

In a large bowl, stir together 2 cups (500 ml) of the flour, the yeast granules and the salt. Add the hot water and the oil, and stir until everything is well mixed (it will be sticky and gooey — that's fine). Now add some of the remaining flour, 1/2 cup (125 ml) at a time, stirring it with a wooden spoon until it becomes too thick to stir.

At this point, dump about 1/2 cup (125 ml) of the remaining flour onto a flat surface (a table, counter, large cutting board) and turn the sticky lump of dough out onto this floured surface. Begin to knead. This is the fun part. Squash the dough down with the heel of your hand, while turning and folding, over and over again, for 8 to 10 minutes. If the dough sticks to the counter, sprinkle with a little more flour. How do you know when the dough is ready? Pinch it gently between your fingers — when it feels like your earlobe, it's done. It should be smooth and stretchy and no longer stick on the surface. You may not need to use all the flour.

Place the dough in an oiled bowl and turn it in the bowl to make sure all the sides are coated with oil. Cover with plastic wrap and place in a warm spot to rise until double in volume — about 30 minutes, more or less.

When the dough has doubled in size, admire it for a moment, then make a fist and punch the dough right in the gizzard to deflate it. Turn it out of the bowl, knead it 2 or 3 times and set it aside while you prepare to create something wonderful.

Makes enough dough for two 12-inch (30 cm) pizzas or two 8 or 9-inch (20 or 23 cm) Fabulous Focaccia breads.

There. Wasn't that fun?

# Fabulous Focaccia

Focaccia is an addictive flatbread — a little like pizza, only breadier. If you've never made bread before, this is an easy place to start. Start with one recipe of Italian Everything Dough (see page 159) and see where it takes you.

Prepare Italian Everything Dough. Let the dough rise, punch it down, then let it rest for about 5 minutes while you grease two 8 or 9-inch (20 or 23 cm) round cake pans (or a couple of cookie sheets) and get your toppings ready. Preheat the oven to 375°F (190°C).

Working with half of the dough at a time, roll it out on a lightly floured surface and place it in the prepared baking pan. Arrange toppings (see below for some possibilities) on top of the dough. Repeat with second half of dough and the same toppings or a different combo, then cover both pans loosely with plastic wrap and let rise again until almost double — 20 to 30 minutes.

When they're puffed and risen, place in the preheated oven and bake for 25 to 30 minutes, or until the dough is lightly browned on the edges and the center is no longer gooey (stick a fork into it to check).

Just try and resist eating the whole thing immediately.

Makes 2 Fabulous Focaccias.

## Focaccia variations

**Perfectly Simple:** Sauté an onion or two with some chopped garlic in olive oil. Arrange sautéed onions on top of dough and sprinkle with a little grated Parmesan cheese, some fresh or dried oregano or rosemary and salt and pepper.

**Mainly Mediterranean:** Sprinkle the rolled-out dough with chopped black olives and sun-dried tomatoes, a little crumbled feta cheese and some salt, pepper and rosemary.

**Somewhat Sicilian:** Top the rolled-out dough with chopped fresh tomatoes, chopped onion and garlic, and a sprinkle of salt, pepper and grated Parmesan cheese.

**Not Quite Naked:** Brush the top of the dough generously with olive oil, then sprinkle with minced fresh garlic, salt, pepper and rosemary or oregano.

# Honey Wheat Bread

*Everyone should know how to make a loaf of bread and this simple recipe is a good place to start. It makes one excellent loaf that's perfect for sandwiches or just to show off how brilliant you are.*

2½ cups (625 ml) all-purpose flour, divided (approximately)
1 cup (250 ml) whole wheat flour
1 envelope quick-rise instant yeast (2¼ tsp./11 ml) granules
1 tsp. (5 ml) salt
1 cup (250 ml) milk
¼ cup (60 ml) water
¼ cup (60 ml) honey
1 tbsp. (15 ml) butter

In a large bowl, stir together 1 1/2 cups (375 ml) of the all-purpose flour, all the whole wheat flour, the yeast and the salt.

In a small saucepan, combine the milk, water, honey and butter, and heat it over medium heat until just hot to the touch — not boiling.

Add the hot milk mixture to the flour mixture and stir with a wooden spoon — it may be sticky and gooey. Add 1/2 cup (125 ml) of the remaining flour, mixing it until the mixture becomes too hard to stir.

There should still be some flour left. Sprinkle just a little of it on your table or counter or another flat surface you can use for kneading the dough. Turn the dough out onto this surface and begin kneading. Press the dough down with the heel of your hand, while turning and folding, over and over again, for 8 to 10 minutes. If the dough sticks to the counter, sprinkle with a little more flour. How do you know when the dough is ready? Pinch it gently between your fingers —when it feels like your earlobe, it's done. It should be smooth, stretchy and no longer sticky on the surface. You may not use the entire amount of flour — that's fine.

Lightly oil a large bowl. Place the dough into the bowl and turn it over to grease all the sides. Cover with plastic wrap and place in a warm spot to rise until doubled in size — about 45 minutes to 1 hour. Judge the dough by its size, not by the amount of time — depending on temperature and the mood of the yeast (we're convinced it gets moody), it can take a longer or shorter time to rise to double.

Preheat the oven to 375°F (190°C). Grease a 9 x 5-inch (23 x 13 cm) loaf pan.

Remove the plastic wrap from the bowl of dough. Punch your fist into the middle of the dough (oh, this is so satisfying to do) to deflate it. Knead it a few times, just to let it know who's boss, and then gently form it into a loaf shape and place it in the prepared pan. (Now tell it you're sorry for beating it up.) Cover loosely with plastic wrap, put it back into its warm, cozy rising spot and let it rise again — this time for about 30 minutes, or until almost double in size. (The second rise is always faster.)

Uncover the pan and place it in the preheated oven — bake for 30 to 35 minutes, or until the loaf is golden brown on top and sounds hollow when you tap on it. If you're not quite sure, give it another 5 minutes and check again.

Remove your perfectly gorgeous bread from the pan, and for heaven's sake, have the decency to let it cool for at least a few minutes before eating it.

Did you do that? Wow.

Makes 1 loaf.

# Go-with-Anything Biscuits

*For breakfast, with jam. For lunch, with ham and cheese. For dinner, with soup. There is no bad time for homemade biscuits.*

2 cups (500 ml) all-purpose flour
1 tbsp. (15 ml) baking powder
1 tsp. (5 ml) granulated sugar
½ tsp. (2 ml) salt
⅓ cup (75 ml) cold butter, cut into chunks
¾ cup (175 ml) milk

Preheat the oven to 425°F (220°C). Line a cookie sheet with parchment paper.

If you have a food processor, measure the flour, baking powder, sugar and salt into the container of the machine. Add the butter chunks and mix the butter into the flour with quick on/off pulses — just so the butter is in tiny pieces mixed through the flour and the whole business looks a little like oatmeal. Transfer to a bowl.

If you don't have a processor, cut the butter chunks into the flour using two knives or a pastry blender utensil, chopping it into smaller and smaller bits until the mixture looks like oatmeal.

Either way, stir the milk into the flour/butter mixture by hand, stirring just until it comes together as a dough. Dump onto a floured surface (a table or cutting board) and knead lightly 4 or 5 times, just until it becomes smoothish and can be rolled out.

Roll or pat the dough out onto a floured surface until it's about 1/2 inch (1 cm) thick. With a 2-inch (5 cm) round cookie cutter (or a glass about that size), cut rounds of dough and arrange them on the cookie sheet. Re-form the scraps and continue until you've used up all the dough. (This makes quite a small and dainty biscuit — if you want them bigger, use a bigger cutter.)

Bake in the preheated oven for 12 to 14 minutes, until lightly browned on top and nicely puffed.

Serve warm. With anything.

Makes 10 to 12 biscuits.

## Cheese, please!

Add 1 cup (250 ml) shredded cheddar (or whatever cheese you have) to the dry mixture after you've cut in the butter but before adding the milk. Everything else remains the same. Yes, these are amazing.

# Blender Banana Bread

*You know those bananas you forgot to eat? The black ones? Give them another chance — make some banana bread.*

1¼ cups (300 ml) all-purpose flour
¾ cup (175 ml) granulated sugar
1 tsp. (5 ml) baking powder
½ tsp. (2 ml) baking soda
½ cup (125 ml) vegetable oil
2 seriously ripe bananas, peeled
2 eggs

Preheat the oven to 350°F (180°C). Grease a 9 x 5-inch (23 x 13 cm) loaf pan.

In a large bowl, mix the flour, sugar, baking powder and baking soda.

Put the oil, bananas and eggs into the container of a blender and blend until smooth. Add the banana mixture to the flour mixture in the bowl and stir until well mixed and smooth. Spoon into the prepared loaf pan and bake for 55 minutes to 1 hour, or until golden brown and a toothpick poked into the middle of the loaf comes out clean (with no batter clinging to it).

Makes 1 perfect banana bread.

## Muffin alternative

Use the same batter to make banana muffins, if you prefer. Grease the cups of a muffin pan or line with paper liners. Fill cups to within 1/4 inch (.5 cm) of the top and bake for about 30 minutes, or until a toothpick poked into the middle of one muffin comes out clean (with no batter clinging to it).

### Go nuts

Chocolate chips? Raisins? Nuts? Go ahead and add ½ to 1 cup (125 to 250 ml) of any of them to the basic banana bread batter. You may never want to go plain again.

# Desserts, Cookies, Cakes and Pie (Oh My!)

Sure, your guests will be polite enough through dinner. But let's be honest — we know they're all really waiting for dessert. Don't disappoint them.

# Baked Apples

*A nice, squishy baked apple is a very sensible dessert. But it's nothing that a little ice cream can't fix. Have both. You've earned it.*

4 medium apples (Macintosh, Spy, Cortland and Idared are good apples for
   baking, but you can experiment with whatever is available)
¼ cup (60 ml) light brown sugar
¼ tsp. (1 ml) cinnamon
2 tbsp. (30 ml) butter
¼ cup (60 ml) boiling water

Preheat the oven to 375°F (190°C). Grease a baking dish just big enough to hold the 4 apples comfortably.

Wash the apples, then core them from the stem end down, almost but *not quite* all the way through to the bottom. You want to leave the bottom intact to contain the fillings. Pull out the cores and discard. With a sharp knife, cut a shallow slit horizontally through the skin around the equator of each apple, about 1/3 of the way down from the top — this prevents the apple from splitting when it bakes. Arrange apples, cavity-side up, in the prepared baking dish.

In a small bowl, combine the sugar and cinnamon. Fill the cavity of each apple with the sugar mixture, dividing it equally among the apples. Plug the top with a dab of butter.

Pour the boiling water into the dish around the apples, place in the preheated oven and bake for 30 to 40 minutes, or until very tender, basting every so often with the liquid in the pan.

Let the apples cool slightly before serving, then serve warm or at room temperature with ice cream, or just plain with a spoonful of the baking liquid drizzled over top.

# Bananas Flambé

*Now this is fun. Really fun. That it also happens to be a crazy delicious dessert is almost beside the point. But if the idea of setting fire to your dessert makes you nervous, this will still be excellent without the flambéing step, so you can skip it if you want.*

4 large, ripe bananas, peeled and cut in half crosswise, then split in half
   lengthwise (making 4 pieces from each banana)
2 tsp. (10 ml) lemon juice
3 tbsp. (45 ml) butter
½ cup (125 ml) light brown sugar
3 tbsp. (45 ml) brandy or liqueur, any kind
Vanilla ice cream

Sprinkle the cut bananas with the lemon juice to prevent them from turning brown and place them in a bowl.

Melt the butter in a large skillet over medium heat, add the brown sugar and stir well. Add the bananas to the pan and cook for about 3 minutes, or until almost tender, turning them over carefully once — they should be golden brown and quite soft but still intact. Remove the pan from the heat.

Put on your oven mitts and turn off the lights.

Okay, now here's the good part. Pour the brandy or liqueur over the bananas in the skillet. With a long fireplace match or barbecue lighter, set the bananas on fire. (Make sure your hands are protected and there are no curtains or other things nearby that could ignite.) Enjoy the show while the brandy burns off, and allow the flames to die out by themselves. (Wasn't that exciting?)

Spoon the bananas and syrupy sauce over vanilla ice cream.

Makes 4 thrilling servings.

# Antidepressant Brownies

*You flunked the geography test. You lost your favorite sweater. You had a fight with your best friend. It's raining. You need some brownies — fast.*

1 cup (250 ml) chocolate chips
⅔ cup (150 ml) granulated sugar
⅓ cup (75 ml) butter
2 tbsp. (30 ml) water
2 eggs
¾ cup (175 ml) all-purpose flour
1 tsp. (5 ml) vanilla extract
½ tsp. (2 ml) baking powder
½ cup (125 ml) coarsely chopped walnuts, if desired

Preheat the oven to 350°F (180°C). Grease an 8 or 9-inch (20 or 23 cm) square baking pan.

In a medium saucepan, combine the chocolate chips, sugar, butter and water. Place over low heat and cook, stirring constantly, just until the chocolate is melted and the mixture is smooth. Remove from heat and let cool for at least 5 minutes.

Add the eggs to the chocolate mixture and whisk until smooth. Dump in the flour, vanilla and baking powder, and stir until all the dry ingredients have been incorporated, then stir in the chopped nuts if you're using them. Pour into the prepared baking pan.

Bake in the preheated oven for 25 to 30 minutes — until a toothpick poked into the middle comes out nearly clean. If you're not quite sure, then they're probably done. It's better to underbake these brownies than to overbake them.

Makes 16 to 25 doses — er, brownies.

## Baking powder, baking soda — what's the difference, anyway?

If the recipe calls for baking powder, no, you can't use baking soda instead. Or vice versa. Here's why. When you mix baking soda (also known as sodium bicarbonate) with an acid ingredient (such as vinegar, lemon juice or yogurt), a chemical reaction takes place, creating little carbon dioxide bubbles that make your pancakes or muffins nice and fluffy. Baking powder, on the other hand, is already a mixture of baking soda and an acid, so it bubbles with no help whatsoever. In addition, baking powder also reacts to heat, causing it to double-bubble — first when you mix it into the batter and again when you bake it. The two products work differently and can't be substituted for one another. So pay attention!

# Self-Saucing Hot Fudge Pudding    serves 6

*This is a sort of a gloppy brownie that makes its own chocolate sauce. It's a killer cure for the "I need something chocolate" blues and it's much too easy to make. You've been warned.*

1 cup (250 ml) all-purpose flour
1½ cups (375 ml) granulated sugar, divided
2 tsp. (10 ml) baking powder
½ cup (125 ml) vegetable oil
½ cup (125 ml) unsweetened cocoa powder, divided
½ cup (125 ml) milk
1 tsp. (5 ml) vanilla extract
½ cup (125 ml) chopped walnuts or pecans (optional, but good if you like nuts)
1¾ cups (425 ml) hot water

Preheat the oven to 350°F (180°C). Grease a 9-inch (23 cm) square baking dish.

In the prepared baking dish, stir together the flour, 3/4 cup (175 ml) of the sugar (this is just *half* the total amount of sugar) and the baking powder. In a small bowl, stir together the vegetable oil and 1/4 cup (60 ml) of the cocoa (*half* the total amount of cocoa). Add the cocoa mixture to the flour mixture, along with the milk and the vanilla. Stir with a fork until combined.

In another bowl, stir together the remaining 3/4 cup (175 ml) of the sugar, the remaining 1/4 cup (60 ml) of the cocoa and the chopped nuts, if you're using them. Sprinkle this dry mixture evenly over the batter in the pan — *don't mix it in*. Now carefully pour the hot water over everything — don't mess with it; don't stir it.

Place in the preheated oven and bake for 40 to 45 minutes, or until the top is crusty and a bubbly chocolate sauce has formed in the dish. Let cool for just a few minutes before serving warm with vanilla ice cream (of course).

Makes 6 servings. But I wouldn't count on it.

# Rainy Day Rice Pudding

serves 4

*Though recommended for a rainy day, this rice pudding is also suitable for blinding snowstorms, sleet, even minor hurricanes — as long as the power doesn't go out.*

3 cups (750 ml) milk, heated to very hot (but don't boil)
⅓ cup (75 ml) short grain rice (Arborio or Italian-style rice is best)
¼ cup (60 ml) granulated sugar
2 tbsp. (30 ml) butter
¼ cup (60 ml) raisins (optional)
1 tsp. (5 ml) vanilla extract
Cinnamon for sprinkling

Preheat the oven to 250°F (125°C). Grease an 8-cup (2 liter) ovenproof deep casserole dish.

In a bowl, stir together the milk, rice, sugar and butter. Pour into the prepared casserole dish and place it in the preheated oven. Bake for about 2 1/2 hours, stirring every half hour or so. Add the raisins (if you're using them) and vanilla in the last 30 minutes of baking time.

Remove from the oven, let cool slightly and serve warm. Or chill and serve cold. Sprinkle each serving with a bit of cinnamon and eat while sitting in a comfy chair, watching the rain drip down the window.

# Butterscotch Granola Blondies

*Use any kind of granola you happen to have in the house to make these chewy, delicious bars. They're the perfect way to deploy that leftover, stale stuff at the bottom of the box.*

1 cup (250 ml) light brown sugar
¼ cup (60 ml) butter, melted
1 egg
2 tsp. (10 ml) vanilla extract
¾ cup (175 ml) all-purpose flour
1 tsp. (5 ml) baking powder
1 cup (250 ml) granola cereal

Preheat the oven to 350°F (180°C). Grease an 8 or 9-inch (20 or 23 cm) square baking pan.

In a medium bowl, combine the brown sugar, butter, egg and vanilla. Beat or whisk together until well mixed. Add the flour, baking powder and granola, and stir just until the dry ingredients have been incorporated into the batter. It will be thick. Spread batter in the prepared baking pan. Place in the preheated oven and bake for 25 to 30 minutes, or until lightly browned on the edges. Cut into squares while still warm.

Makes 16 to 25 blondies.

# Fancy French Lemon Tart serves 6–8

*Incredibly easy, very lemony and terribly French.*

1 cup (250 ml) granulated sugar
½ cup (125 ml) lemon juice (about 2 large lemons)
4 eggs
½ cup (125 ml) whipping cream
1 unbaked 9-inch (23 cm) pastry shell
Icing sugar for dusting the top
Whipped cream and berries for serving (optional)

Preheat the oven to 375°F (190°C). Have the unbaked pastry shell ready to fill.

In a mixing bowl, beat together the sugar, lemon juice and eggs with an electric mixer for about 1 minute. Add the cream and beat until combined. Pour into the pastry shell.

Place on the lowest rack of the preheated oven and bake for 30 to 40 minutes, or until filling is just set in the middle when you jiggle the pan — it will still be a bit wet (that's fine). Remove from oven and let cool completely.

Just before serving, dust the top with icing sugar. A dollop of whipped cream and a few fresh berries are also nice, but not absolutely necessary.

Makes one 9-inch (23 cm) tart — 6 to 8 servings.

# Fruit Crumble

serves 6–8

*Apples are probably the most crumbled fruit, but this is also excellent when made with peaches or rhubarb or blueberries or pears or plums. Or go crazy and try a combination of whatever you have in the house. (See below for ideas.) You can use frozen fruit if you want — don't thaw before using.*

## Fruit mixture

4 cups (1 liter) prepared fruit (peeled, cored, pitted, cut into chunks or slices — whatever is appropriate for the fruit you're using)
½ cup (125 ml) granulated sugar
3 tbsp. (45 ml) cornstarch

## Crumble topping

1 cup (250 ml) all-purpose flour
½ cup (125 ml) butter
½ cup (125 ml) light brown sugar
½ tsp. (2 ml) cinnamon

Preheat the oven to 375°F (190°C). Grease an 8 or 9-inch (20 or 23 cm) square baking pan.

In a large bowl, toss the fruit with the sugar and cornstarch. You may want to adjust the amount of sugar to suit your taste and the sweetness of the fruit (rhubarb will need more sugar than ripe peaches will). Dump into the prepared baking pan.

In a large bowl, combine all the ingredients for the crumble topping — the flour, butter, brown sugar and cinnamon. Smush everything together using a fork or pastry blender utensil until it forms a slightly sticky, crumbly mixture. Sprinkle this crumble topping evenly over the fruit in the baking pan.

Place in the preheated oven and bake for 35 to 45 minutes, or until the fruit bubbles around the edges of the pan and the topping is lightly browned. Let cool for a few minutes. You must serve this warm with vanilla ice cream. It's the law.

## Crumbly possibilities

**Apples, peaches, pears:** Peel, core (or pit) and cut into slices or chunks.
**Berries:** Wash and remove stems. Cut in half or leave whole.
**Plums, cherries:** Remove pits and cut into chunks if necessary.
**Rhubarb:** Wash and cut into 1/2-inch (1 cm) pieces.

# Chocolate Mousse

*You + chocolate + 10 minutes = the most insanely delicious chocolate mousse imaginable.*

¼ cup (60 ml) water
3 tbsp. (45 ml) granulated sugar
1 cup (250 ml) semisweet chocolate chips
1 cup (250 ml) whipping cream
**Additional whipped cream and chocolate shavings or berries for serving**

Place the water and sugar in a small saucepan over medium heat and bring to a boil. Remove from heat, add the chocolate chips and let the mixture sit for 2 or 3 minutes to allow the chocolate to soften. Stir until the chocolate is melted and the mixture is smooth. Transfer to a medium-size bowl and let cool to room temperature.

In a mixing bowl, with an electric mixer, beat the whipping cream until it is thick and fluffy and holds soft peaks.

With the electric mixer, briefly beat the cooled chocolate mixture (it will have thickened) until smooth. By hand, stir in a spoonful of the whipped cream to lighten the mixture. Then fold in the remaining whipped cream and mix gently until it's evenly incorporated. (There may be a few white streaks, but don't worry about it.) Spoon mousse into 4 serving dishes and chill for about an hour.

Garnish each serving with a blob of whipped cream and some chocolate shavings or a few berries. Fantastic!

# Crème Caramel

*You want to make a sophisticated dessert — elegant, understated. Something French-ish and impressive. Something that appears tricky to create — but isn't. Here you go.*

¾ cup (175 ml) granulated sugar, divided
3 eggs
2½ cups (625 ml) milk, heated until hot but not boiling
½ tsp. (2 ml) vanilla extract

Preheat the oven to 350°F (180°C). Have ready six 1/2-cup (125 ml) glass or ceramic custard cups. Arrange these in a baking pan large enough to hold them all comfortably.

In your smallest, heaviest saucepan, heat 1/2 cup (125 ml) of the sugar over medium heat, stirring constantly. At first the sugar does nothing. Then it starts to go clumpy and weird. And then — amazingly — the sugar melts and turns into a golden syrup. Don't try to hurry this process, because sugar burns easily. Remove the pan from the heat as soon as the syrup turns golden and pour it into the custard cups, dividing the syrup evenly among the cups and swirling them so the syrup coats the bottoms and sides. The caramelized-sugar syrup will solidify as it cools. Set aside.

Beat the eggs in a mixing bowl with the remaining 1/4 cup (60 ml) of the sugar. Add the hot milk and vanilla, and stir until the sugar is dissolved. Pour into the caramel-lined custard cups, dividing the mixture evenly.

Boil some water in a saucepan or kettle. Pour this boiling water carefully into the baking pan in which the custard cups are sitting — the water should come about halfway up the sides of the cups. (You are creating a water bath around the custard cups so that they bake slowly and evenly.) Put the entire pan — water and custard cups — into the preheated oven and bake for 50 minutes to 1 hour, or until a knife poked into the middle of one of the cups comes out clean, with nothing stuck to it.

Cool your crème caramels to room temperature, then refrigerate for several hours or, preferably, overnight. When you're ready to serve, run a thin knife around the edge of each custard to loosen it from its cup. Place a plate over top and flip over to unmold each one gently. During the baking and chilling process the caramelized sugar with have magically liquefied into a sauce, which you should spoon over the plated custards. Repeat with the remaining custards.

Take a bow.

# Official Peanut Butter Cookies

*Remember when you were little and your mom used to greet you with a plate of peanut butter cookies and a glass of milk when you came home from school? No? Did anyone's mom ever do that? Well, you'll just have to make them for yourself then, won't you?*

½ cup (125 ml) butter, softened
½ cup (125 ml) peanut butter, smooth or crunchy
½ cup (125 ml) granulated sugar
½ cup (125 ml) light brown sugar
1 egg
1¼ cups (300 ml) all-purpose flour (or whole wheat flour, if you prefer)
½ tsp. (2 ml) baking powder
½ tsp. (2 ml) baking soda
½ cup (125 ml) semisweet chocolate chips (optional, but recommended)

Preheat the oven to 375°F (190°C). Line a cookie sheet or two with aluminum foil or baking parchment paper.

In a large bowl, with an electric mixer, beat together the butter, peanut butter, granulated sugar, brown sugar and egg until smooth and creamy. Add the flour, baking powder and baking soda, and mix until smooth.

By hand, roll the dough into 1-inch (2 cm) balls and place them on the prepared cookie sheets, 2 inches (5 cm) apart. Now here's the crucial step: flatten each ball in a crisscross pattern by pressing down with a fork. This detail is what makes them *official* peanut butter cookies. Do not, under any circumstances, forget to do this.

Finally, if you haven't eaten all the chocolate chips, press 3 or 4 into each cookie, if you want.

Bake in the preheated oven for 10 to 12 minutes, or until golden brown. The cookies will still be a bit soft, but they'll get crisp as they cool.

Makes about 3 1/2 dozen cookies.

# Classic Chocolate Chip Cookies

*Few things on this planet can come even remotely close to the wonderfulness of a homemade chocolate chip cookie. Why don't you make a batch right now? You know you want to.*

1 cup (250 ml) butter, softened
¾ cup (175 ml) granulated sugar
¾ cup (175 ml) light brown sugar
2 eggs
1 tsp. (5 ml) vanilla extract
2¼ cups (550 ml) all-purpose flour
1 tsp. (5 ml) baking soda
¼ tsp. (1 ml) salt
2 cups (500 ml) semisweet chocolate
  chips
1 cup (250 ml) chopped walnuts or
  pecans (optional)

Preheat the oven to 375°F (190°C). Have ready one or two cookie sheets, but don't grease them.

In a large bowl, with an electric mixer, beat the butter with the granulated sugar, brown sugar, eggs and vanilla until nice and creamy.

In another bowl, combine the flour with the baking soda and salt. Add to the butter mixture and beat until everything is smooth and blended. Stir in the chocolate chips by hand. At this point, certain people might add nuts. We're not judging.

Drop the dough by teaspoonfuls onto the ungreased cookie sheet, about 2 inches (5 cm) apart. Don't crowd the cookies — the baking time is short and you'll be baking several batches. Place in the preheated oven and bake for 10 to 12 minutes, or until the edges are just browned but the cookies are still a little soft in the middle. With a spatula, carefully remove the cookies to a cooling rack and repeat with the remaining dough. (If you have two cookie sheets, you can prepare one batch while the other one is baking.)

Try not to eat all the cookies before they're cool. Also share. It's the right thing to do.

Makes 6 to 8 dozen, depending on the size and how much dough you ate.

# Classic Carrot Cake

*Who else but a mom would possibly have thought to put carrots in a cake and cream cheese in the frosting? This is a classic.*

2 cups (500 ml) all-purpose flour
2 tsp. (10 ml) baking powder
1½ tsp. (7 ml) baking soda
1 tsp. (5 ml) cinnamon
2 cups (500 ml) granulated sugar
1 cup (250 ml) vegetable oil
4 eggs
2 cups (500 ml) grated carrots (about 3 medium carrots)
1 cup (250 ml) canned unsweetened crushed pineapple, well drained
½ cup (125 ml) chopped walnuts or pecans

Preheat the oven to 350°F (180°C). Line the bottoms of two 8 or 9-inch (20 or 23 cm) round cake pans or one 9 x 13-inch (23 x 33 cm) rectangular cake pan with baking parchment paper. Grease the paper and the sides of the pans.

In a medium bowl, stir together the flour, baking powder, baking soda and cinnamon.

In a large bowl, with an electric mixer, beat the sugar, oil and eggs until smooth. Add the flour mixture to the egg mixture and beat until well blended. By hand, stir in the carrots, pineapple and nuts, mixing until everything is evenly combined. Pour the batter into the prepared baking pans.

Bake in the preheated oven for 40 to 45 minutes, until a toothpick poked into the middle of the cake comes out clean. Remove from the oven and let cool for about 5 minutes. Run a knife around the sides of the cake to loosen it from the pan, then turn the layers out onto a cooling rack. Peel off the paper and let cool completely before frosting with Cream Cheese Frosting (see recipe on page 184).

Makes two 8 or 9-inch (20 or 23 cm) round layers or one 9 x 13-inch (23 x 33 cm) rectangular cake.

# Idiotproof One-Bowl Chocolate Cake

*It's probably possible to mess up this easy cake, but you'd really have to work at it. And why on earth would anyone do such a thing? This cake is dark, rich and perfect.*

2 cups (500 ml) all-purpose flour
2 cups (500 ml) granulated sugar
½ cup (125 ml) unsweetened cocoa powder
1 tsp. (5 ml) baking powder
1 tsp. (5 ml) baking soda
1½ cups (375 ml) milk
½ cup (125 ml) vegetable oil
1 tsp. (5 ml) vanilla extract
2 eggs

Preheat the oven to 350°F (180°C). Line the bottoms of two 8 or 9-inch (20 or 23 cm) round cake pans or one 9 x 13-inch (23 x 33 cm) rectangular cake pan with baking parchment paper. Grease the paper and the sides of the pans.

In a large mixing bowl, whisk together the flour, sugar, cocoa powder, baking powder and baking soda. Add the milk, vegetable oil and vanilla, and beat with an electric mixer for about 2 minutes, until smooth, scraping down the sides of the bowl several times. Add the eggs and beat for another minute or two. Pour batter into the prepared pans.

Bake in the preheated oven for 35 to 40 minutes, or until a toothpick poked into the middle of the cake comes out clean. Let cool in the pan for 5 minutes, then run a knife around the edges of the pan to loosen the cake, and invert it onto a cooling rack. Peel off the paper and let cool completely before frosting.

Makes two 8 or 9-inch (20 or 23 cm) round layers or one 9 x 13-inch (23 x 33 cm) rectangular cake.

# Idiotproof One-Bowl Yellow Cake

*Ridiculously easy, light and delicious — this cake can handle whatever you care to throw at it. Especially strawberries and whipped cream.*

2 cups (500 ml) granulated sugar
4 eggs

¾ cup (175 ml) vegetable oil
1 cup (250 ml) milk
2½ cups (600 ml) all-purpose flour
2¼ tsp. (11 ml) baking powder
1 tsp. (5 ml) vanilla extract

Preheat the oven to 350°F (180°C). Line the bottoms of two 8 or 9-inch (20 or 23 cm) round cake pans or one 9 x 13-inch (23 x 33 cm) rectangular cake pan with baking parchment paper. Grease the paper and the sides of the pans.

In a large mixing bowl, beat the sugar and eggs with an electric mixer until slightly thickened — about 1 minute. Add the oil, milk, flour, baking powder and vanilla, and beat for 1 more minute — just until the batter is smooth and creamy. Don't overbeat it. Pour batter into the prepared pans.

Bake in the preheated oven for 30 to 35 minutes, until the tops are golden brown and a toothpick poked into the center of the cake comes out clean. Let cool in the pan for 5 minutes, then run a knife around the sides of the cake to loosen it from the pan. Turn the cake out onto a cooling rack, peel off the paper and let cool completely before frosting.

Makes two 8 or 9-inch (20 or 23 cm) round layers or one 9 x 13-inch (23 x 33 cm) rectangular cake.

# Foolproof Banana Cake

*Crazy easy and stupid delicious. Use the ripest, squishiest bananas you can find to make this.*

1½ cups (375 ml) mashed bananas (4 or 5 medium bananas)
1¼ cups (300 ml) granulated sugar
2 eggs
½ cup (125 ml) vegetable oil
2 cups (500 ml) all-purpose flour
2½ tsp. (12 ml) baking powder
½ tsp. (2 ml) baking soda
1 cup (250 ml) semisweet chocolate chips (optional)

Preheat the oven to 350°F (180°C). Line the bottoms of two 8 or 9-inch (20 or 23 cm) round cake pans or one 9 x 13-inch (23 x 33 cm) rectangular cake pan with baking parchment paper. Grease the paper and the sides of the pans.

In a large bowl, beat together the mashed bananas, sugar, eggs and oil.

In another bowl, whisk together the flour, baking powder and baking soda. Add the flour mixture to the banana mixture and beat with an electric mixer until smooth. If you want to add the chocolate chips, stir them in now. Dump batter into the prepared baking pan.

Bake in the preheated oven for 30 to 35 minutes, or until a toothpick poked into the middle of the cake comes out clean. Let cool for 5 minutes, then run a knife around the sides of the cake to loosen it from the pan. Turn the cake out onto a cooling rack, peel off the paper and let cool completely before frosting with whatever frosting seems most delicious to you at the moment.

Makes two 8 or 9-inch (20 or 23 cm) round layers or one 9 x 13-inch (23 x 33 cm) rectangular cake.

# Speedy Apple Cake                                    serves 4–6

*Here's a fast, goofproof dessert that's guaranteed to make everyone happy (except grumpy old Uncle Fred, who, let's face it, doesn't like anything). Serve with a dollop of whipped cream for extra deliciousness.*

3 medium apples, peeled, cored and thinly sliced (4 cups/1 liter sliced apples)
¾ cup (175 ml) granulated sugar, divided
1 tsp. (5 ml) cinnamon
2 tbsp. (30 ml) butter, softened
1 egg
½ cup (125 ml) all-purpose flour
1 tsp. (5 ml) baking powder

Preheat the oven to 350°F (180°C). Grease a 9-inch (23 cm) pie pan or other baking dish.

Dump the sliced apples into the prepared pie pan and sprinkle with 1/4 cup (60 ml) of the sugar and all the cinnamon.

In a mixing bowl, with an electric mixer, beat together the butter and the remaining 1/2 cup (125 ml) sugar. Add the egg and mix well, then add the flour and baking powder. Beat until smooth. Drop this batter by spoonfuls over the apples. There won't be quite enough batter to cover the apples completely — that's okay. Just leave part of the apples exposed (*eek!*).

Place in the preheated oven and bake for 40 to 45 minutes, or until the apples are soft and the cake is browned.

There. Dessert just doesn't get much easier. Don't forget the whipped cream.

# Desperate for Cheesecake

*If this cheesecake is too much work for you, then you're obviously not desperate enough. Yet.*

## Crust
1½ cups (375 ml) graham cracker crumbs
¼ cup (60 ml) melted butter
¼ cup (60 ml) granulated sugar

## Filling
2 pkg. (8 oz./250 g each) cream cheese, softened
½ cup (125 ml) granulated sugar
1 tsp. (5 ml) vanilla extract
2 eggs

Preheat the oven to 350°F (180°C).

First, make the crust. In a bowl, stir together the crust ingredients: the graham cracker crumbs, melted butter and sugar. Press firmly and evenly into the bottom and up the sides of a 9-inch (23 cm) pie pan. If you happen to own two pie pans, you can use the second one to squish the crumb mixture into the first one to help get the crust smooth and even. Set aside.

Now make the filling. In a large bowl, with an electric mixer, beat together the cream cheese, sugar and vanilla until well blended. Add the eggs, one at a time, and keep beating for another couple of minutes, until the filling is smooth and creamy. Pour into the graham cracker crust.

Place in the preheated oven and bake for 40 to 45 minutes, until just set. The center of the cheesecake should still be a bit soft and wobbly, so don't overbake it. It will firm up as it cools. Refrigerate for at least 3 hours (or as long as overnight) before serving.

Top with fresh fruit (like strawberries, blueberries or peaches) or your favorite ready-made pie filling. Purists, of course, may prefer their cheesecake left plain. To each his own.

# Frostings (not from a can)

So there you are. You've made a cake from scratch. You're feeling very proud of yourself — and rightly so. Now, are you really going to use canned frosting? We think not.

Each of these recipes will make enough frosting to fill and frost one two-layer 8 or 9-inch (20 or 23 cm) cake or the top of one 9 x 13-inch (23 x 33 cm) rectangular cake. And there's no law that says you can't use them on cupcakes.

## Chocolate Frosting

½ cup (125 ml) butter, softened
4 cups (1 liter) icing sugar
½ cup (125 ml) unsweetened cocoa powder
1 tsp. (5 ml) vanilla extract
½ cup (125 ml) milk

In a large bowl, beat the butter with an electric mixer until creamy. Add the icing sugar, cocoa, vanilla and 1/4 cup (60 ml) of the milk, and beat until the mixture begins to get clumpy. It will still be quite dry. Now add the remaining 1/4 cup (60 ml) milk and continue beating until the frosting is creamy, fluffy and absolutely perfect.

## Vanilla Frosting

½ cup (125 ml) butter
3 cups (750 ml) icing sugar
2 tsp. (10 ml) vanilla extract
½ cup (125 ml) milk

In a large bowl, beat the butter with an electric mixer until creamy. Add the icing sugar, vanilla and 1/4 cup (60 ml) of the milk, and beat until the mixture begins to clump up — it will still be quite dry. Add the remaining milk and continue beating until the frosting is smooth and creamy.

## Cream Cheese Frosting

4 cups (1 liter) icing sugar
1 cup (250 ml) cream cheese, softened
½ cup (125 ml) butter, softened

Combine everything in a large bowl and beat until smooth and creamy. Done.

# An Actual Pie Made by You

See — it's not so hard.

1 recipe Foolproof Pastry Dough (see recipe on page 186)
1 batch prepared fruit filling (see page 188 for options)

Preheat the oven to 375°F (190°C). Have ready a 9-inch (23 cm) pie pan.

Roll out 1 ball of pastry dough (half the recipe) on a well-floured surface to a circle about 12 inches (30 cm) in diameter. Sprinkle as much flour underneath the dough as you need to keep it from sticking on the bottom as you roll. The edges may be a little rough — don't worry about it. Carefully fold the rolled dough in half and gently lift it into the pie pan. Unfold and fit it evenly into the pan without stretching it. Some dough will overhang the edges — this is good. With a sharp knife, cut the dough even with the rim of the pan.

In a large bowl, prepare your fruit filling. Dump it into the crust, mounding the fruit higher in the middle than around the sides.

Now roll out the second ball of pastry dough, again on a well-floured surface, in a circle about the same size as the first one. Fold the pastry in half, lift it up carefully and gently center it over the filled crust. Unfold so that it covers the filling and let the edges drape over the sides. Leaving a small amount of overhang, trim the excess pastry so that it's even all around. Now, very gently, tuck the edges of the top crust under the edges of the bottom crust — as if you were tucking the top sheet in when making a bed. This keeps everything enclosed in pastry and helps prevent leaks. With your fingers, firmly pinch the edges all around to make a frilly-looking border or press all around the edges with the tines of a fork. Cut 3 or 4 slits in the top of the crust as steam vents. Put the finished pie on a larger cookie sheet or pizza pan (to catch any messy boil-overs in the oven).

Place the pie in the preheated oven and bake for 50 to 60 minutes, or until the fruit is tender and bubbling. Poke a knife in through one of the steam vents to check on the doneness of the fruit.

Wow — did *you* make that?

## Make mine crumbly

Instead of fully enclosing your homemade pie in a double crust — top *and* bottom — you can top the fruit with a crumbly mixture. Use the same crumble topping from the Fruit Crumble recipe on page 174 in place of a top crust. Just sprinkle it on and bake as usual.

## How to measure butter

Measuring butter is one of those stupid jobs that no one likes to do. The butter sticks to the cup, it doesn't pack down easily, it's just annoying. Here's a trick to make the job easier.

Let's say your recipe requires ½ cup (125 ml) of butter. Fill a measuring cup to the ½ cup (125 ml) level with cold (important detail!) water. Scoop in the butter, any which way, until it fills the cup all the way to the 1-cup (250 ml) mark. Drain off the water as well as possible and voilà! You now have ½ cup (125 ml) of butter.

Obviously, different quantities of butter will require you to do a little math. But it will work.

You can also use this trick to measure other solid fats, such as vegetable shortening, margarine or lard.

# Foolproof Pastry Dough

*If you have a food processor, you can make this dough in about 10 minutes flat. Without one, it might take half an hour, but it's totally worth the effort.*

2½ cups (625 ml) all-purpose flour, divided
2 tbsp. (30 ml) granulated sugar
¼ tsp. (1 ml) salt
¾ cup (175 ml) cold butter, cut into chunks
½ cup (125 ml) cold vegetable shortening, cut into chunks
½ cup (125 ml) water

*If you have a food processor,* place 1 1/2 cups (375 ml) of the flour, the sugar and salt into the bowl of the machine. Process to mix. Add the butter and shortening, and process, by pulsing the machine on and off, until the dough just starts to collect in uneven clumps — it will look like cottage cheese. Scrape the bowl down and add the remaining 1 cup (250 ml) of flour. Process briefly, just until it forms a crumbly mixture. Dump into a bowl.

*If you don't have a processor,* mix 1 1/2 cups (375 ml) of the flour, the sugar and salt in a large bowl. Add the butter and shortening, and, using two knives or a pastry blender utensil, cut the butter and shortening into the flour mixture until it forms a clumpy, uneven dough. Add the remaining 1 cup (250 ml) of flour and continue to cut the fat into the flour, until the mixture forms finer crumbs and looks like oatmeal.

Either way, now you're ready to add the water. Sprinkle the water over the flour mixture and mix everything with a spatula or wooden spoon, until the whole mess sticks together as a dough. Don't overmix — just form the dough into two equal balls and press them into thick disks.

Wrap dough in plastic wrap and refrigerate for at least 1 hour. You can refrigerate this dough for up to 3 or 4 days or freeze it for longer storage.

Makes 2 single pastry crusts — enough for one double-crust pie.

## Fruit pie fillings

**Apple**
- 5 cups (1.25 liters) peeled, cored and thinly sliced apples (you can use any variety of apple except Red Delicious)
- ¾ cup (175 ml) granulated sugar
- 2 tbsp. (30 ml) all-purpose flour
- 1 tbsp. (15 ml) lemon juice
- ½ tsp. (2 ml) cinnamon

**Blueberry**
- 5 cups (1.25 liters) blueberries, fresh or frozen (if frozen, don't defrost)
- ¾ cup (175 ml) granulated sugar
- ¼ cup (60 ml) cornstarch
- 1 tbsp. (15 ml) lemon juice

**Peach**
- 5 cups (1.25 liters) peeled, pitted and sliced peaches
- ¾ cup (175 ml) granulated sugar
- 2 tbsp. (30 ml) all-purpose flour
- 2 tbsp. (30 ml) cornstarch
- 1 tbsp. (15 ml) lemon juice

**Rhubarb or Strawberry-Rhubarb**
- 5 cups (1.25 liters) chopped fresh or frozen rhubarb or a mixture of rhubarb and strawberries (if frozen, don't defrost)
- 1 cup (250 ml) granulated sugar
- ¼ cup (60 ml) cornstarch

# Killer Pecan Pie

serves 6–8

*Almost too much. But you can handle it.*

1 cup (250 ml) golden corn syrup
⅔ cup (150 ml) granulated sugar
3 eggs
¼ cup (60 ml) butter, melted
1 tsp. (5 ml) vanilla extract
1 cup (250 ml) coarsely chopped pecans
1 unbaked 9-inch (23 cm) pastry shell

Preheat the oven to 350°F (180°C). Have the unbaked pastry shell ready to fill.

In a large bowl, beat the corn syrup, sugar, eggs, melted butter and vanilla with an electric mixer until slightly thickened — 2 or 3 minutes. Stir in the chopped pecans and pour into the prepared pastry shell.

Place the pan on the lowest rack of the preheated oven and bake for 55 to 60 minutes, or until a knife poked into the center of the filling comes out clean.

Ridiculously easy for something so good, isn't it?

Makes one 9-inch (23 cm) pie — 6 to 8 servings.

## Don't leave well enough alone!

### Chocolate Pecan Pie
Melt 4 squares (1 oz./28 g each) semisweet chocolate with the butter in the basic recipe. Bake as usual. Act nonchalant, if possible.

### Maple Walnut Pie
Substitute pure maple syrup for the corn syrup in the basic recipe. Use walnuts instead of pecans. Seriously great.

# Good to Know!
## Other useful bits and pieces of cooking information

### How to Make a Good Cup of Coffee

There are several good ways to make a cup of coffee, and each method has its rabid fans. Here are three of the most common ways to get your daily dose of caffeine. Pick the one that suits your style. As for the coffee itself, the choices are endless. Buy small amounts of the best coffee you can afford and keep it fresh in a tightly closed container.

### Electric drip coffee

You'll need an electric drip coffeemaker for this. Easy enough to find, even second-hand. You'll also need paper filters that fit your machine.

Place a paper filter in the basket of your machine. Measure about 1 tbsp. (15 ml) finely ground coffee for each cup of coffee you will be making. Add an extra spoonful for good luck. Fill the water reservoir with the correct amount of fresh cold water. Flip the switch and you're done. Nothing to it.

### Manual pour-over coffee

You'll need a cone-shaped filter holder and a glass or thermal carafe for the coffee to drip into. If you get a small single-cup filter holder, you can drip the coffee directly into your mug. Cheap, easy and very portable.

Place the correct-size paper filter in the filter holder and set it over the carafe or mug. Add 1 tbsp. (15 ml) finely ground coffee for each cup of coffee you're making, plus a bit extra (a whole extra spoonful for a full pot, less for a single mug). Boil fresh water in a kettle. Pour just enough water into the coffee filter to wet the grounds, let it soak in for 30 seconds, then pour the remaining water gradually over the grounds and allow to drip through. Done.

## French press

The only equipment you'll need is a French press coffeepot. This is a glass cylinder with a sort of plunger-filter contraption built into the lid. These often show up at second-hand stores and garage sales.

Boil some water in a kettle. Remove the plunger gizmo from the press pot. For each 8 oz. (250 ml) of water you'll be pouring into the pot, measure 2 tbsp. (30 ml) coarse or medium ground coffee into the bottom of the cylinder. Pour in the boiling water, stir, then gently place the lid contraption on top — don't press it down yet. Let the coffee steep for 4 minutes. After 4 minutes, slowly press the plunger down until it reaches the bottom. The coffee grounds are trapped beneath the filter plunger. Put on your French beret and write a poem while you enjoy *un bon café*.

# How to Make a Nice Cup of Tea

## What kind?

Regular everyday black tea is made from the fermented leaves of the tea bush. Black tea contains caffeine (like coffee) and is what most people think of as tea. It's available in tea bags or loose leaves. You can find all kinds — some with fruit or flavors added, others processed in particular ways. Black tea may be called Orange Pekoe or Earl Grey or Darjeeling or English Breakfast or some other such thing. Try several varieties and discover which you like best.

Green tea is made from leaves that have not been fermented, so the tea retains the green color of the leaves. Green tea is available in tea bags and loose. There are many different kinds of green tea, each with its own flavor and characteristics. Like black tea, green tea contains caffeine.

Herbal teas are made from various herbs, fruits and spices. These are generally caffeine-free and tend to have funky names like Midnight Mango and Nutmeg Nirvana. You're on your own here — there's a lot to choose from.

## Method

Fill your kettle or saucepan with fresh, cold water. Bring it to a full boil. Meanwhile, rinse your cup or teapot out with hot water and, if you're using tea bags, put them in now.

Use 1 tea bag for every 2 cups of boiling water. So, for example, if your teapot holds 4 cups of water, use 2 tea bags. Pour in the boiling water and let the tea steep for 5 minutes. Remove the tea bag(s) before serving.

If you're using loose tea, use 1 tsp. (5 ml) per cup of water. The method is the same as for tea bags, but you'll have to strain out the leaves or pour carefully so that they remain in the bottom of the cup or teapot.

Black tea is usually served with milk and sugar. Some people prefer it with honey and lemon (no milk), and others like it just plain, with nothing. Suit yourself. Herbal tea should be served with honey or sugar or unsweetened, but *never* with milk. And green tea is most often taken straight — no milk, no sugar, no nothing.

# How to Plan a Meal

## The beginning
This is the part of the meal that gets everyone interested and gives the cook time to (madly) finish making the rest of dinner. You might just serve some veggies and dip. Or a bowl of pretzels. Or even beluga caviar on toasts (not bloody likely). Don't go overboard on the starters unless you expect the main course to be inedible or terribly late — and try to avoid serving a food that will appear again later in the meal.

## The middle
Here we have your basic meat-and-potatoes section, where you will generally find your main dish. Of course, it doesn't have to be meat and potatoes. It can be lasagna and salad, beans and rice, or shepherd's pie and broccoli. There's nothing really wrong with the usual formula of one meat thing, one starch thing and one vegetable thing, except that it's not the only way to plan a meal. Try to vary tastes and textures, but don't attempt to make too many different dishes, because you'll drive yourself crazy. And really, one dish with a loaf of good bread is usually more than enough.

Aesthetically speaking, avoid monochromatic meals. A dinner of white chicken, white potatoes and white cauliflower might taste just fine, but it looks really depressing on a plate. An all-black dinner is even worse. And unless it's Saint Patrick's Day, a totally green meal would be just plain weird. Go multicolor.

## The ending
Ah, dessert. The happy ending to a wonderful meal. Or maybe the happy ending to a not-so-great meal. Whatever the story, it's definitely what everyone has been waiting for. Will it be your famous Hot Fudge Pudding? Will it be spectacular Bananas Flambé? Or will it be (drat) sensible, nutritious fruit? Most of the time you'll want to go the sensibly nutritious route. But once in a while something gooey and decadent is very therapeutic. Aim for a balance.

# Cooking Terminology Demystified

Mince, sauté, deglaze — what exactly are they asking us to do, and is it decent?

**Bake**  To cook in an oven. You know — like a cake.

**Baste**  Like when you use sunscreen at the beach. You baste foods like turkey to keep them moist while they're roasting.

**Beat**  To clobber the daylights out of, let's say, an egg. Can be done by hand with a whisk or fork, or with an electric mixer.

**Blend**  To combine ingredients into a uniform mixture.

**Boil**  Scientifically speaking, at sea level, to bring a liquid to 212°F (100°C) until it gets hot and bubbly.

**Chop**  To cut up into little pieces. Bigger than minced, but smaller than diced.

**Cream**  To mush together soft ingredients — like butter and sugar — to make a creamy mixture.

**Curdle**  A disgusting effect that happens to certain sauces or liquids when they are overcooked — yucky, lumpy, separated clumps.

**Dash**  Oh, just a squirt or two.

**Deglaze**  You deglaze a pan by pouring a little liquid into it, then cooking to dissolve the brown bits stuck on the bottom. Makes a nice gravy and cuts down on dishwashing.

**Dice**  Bigger than chopped (see above). Usually in little square-ish shapes.

**Dredge**  To lightly coat a food with flour or crumbs. Who would have guessed?

**Drizzle**  What happens when you forget your umbrella. Just kidding. Actually, to pour a thin stream of liquid over food.

**Drop**  What a person asks for when they really want more. As in "I'll have just another tiny *drop* of lasagna."

**Dunk**  What you do to your chocolate chip cookie in a glass of milk.

**Fold**  To very gently mix one ingredient into another using a spatula to lift from underneath. Don't try to do this when you're in a big hurry.

**Fry**  The f-word. To cook food in a pan with plenty of oil, resulting in either delicious crispness or greasy sog. Depending.

**Garnish**  That little sprig of parsley beside the mashed potatoes. The slice of orange next to the omelet. The paprika on the potato salad. Most commonly found in restaurants where they have time to do this sort of thing.

**Grate**  To put through the holes of a grater, usually resulting in shreddy little pieces. Cheese is the most common victim of this process. Also knuckles. Be careful.

**Grease**  To coat a pan with, yes, grease (butter, vegetable oil or shortening, non-stick cooking spray) so that food doesn't stick.

**Julienne**  Thin strands of any kind of food that doesn't naturally occur in that shape — such as long strings of carrot, zucchini or ham.

**Knead**  To mangle a lump of dough by hand in order to make it smooth and uniform. Usually associated with bread dough. Excellent for venting frustration.

**Leavening**  Any substance that is used to cause a mixture to rise while baking — like yeast or baking powder.

**Marinate**  To soak food in a liquid in order to tenderize it or add flavor.

**Mash**  To squash with a fork or masher. Made famous by potatoes.

**Meringue**  The best part of a lemon pie. A fluffy substance made of stiffly beaten egg whites and sugar.

**Mince**  Smaller than either diced or chopped (see both). Little eensy bits.

**Mix**  Just stir it together, with a spoon or fork or your hands or a shovel. Depending.

**Peel**  To remove the outside of a fruit or vegetable — the part that your mother told you has all the vitamins.

**Pinch**  YOW! Don't do that! Just a tiny bit more than a dash (see above).

**Pit**  To remove the seed, usually of a fruit.

**Poach**  To cook gently in simmering (see below) water or broth.

**Pound**  What you'd like to do to that creep who stole your bike. In food, to flatten.

**Preheat**  To turn your oven on ahead of time, so that it will be at the right temperature when you put the cake in.

**Puree** To mash or blend a solid food into a smooth, lump-free mixture.

**Roast** Really, this is the same as bake (see above), except that it's generally associated with meat. You wouldn't, for example, *roast* a cake.

**Sauté** But of course, zees ees to cook zee food in zee pan weeth just a *petit* leetle bit of zee oil or zee butter. *Ooh la la.*

**Scorch** What happens when you go answer the phone while your spaghetti sauce is boiling, resulting in a black residue on the bottom of the pot, a nasty burned taste and smell and a lot of bad words. Avoid, avoid, avoid!

**Scramble** What you do to an egg with a fork.

**Shred** To cut or grate something into long, thin pieces.

**Sift** What you do to flour in order to remove any lumps and to fluff it up.

**Simmer** Almost boiling, *but not quite.* Tiny little bubbles.

**Sliver** A thin strip. Except when used in the sentence "I'll have just a *sliver* of pumpkin pie," where it actually means a big slice.

**Steam** To cook food in a basket or strainer suspended over (but not touching) boiling water. Especially useful for vegetables.

**Stew** To cook something for a long time in a covered pan with liquid.

**Stir** To mix with a spoon.

**Stir-fry** Tossing and stirring cut-up bits of food in a very hot pan with oil. Very fast, very dramatic. Also very messy if you're not careful.

**Stock** Broth, basically. Can be made with meat or vegetables or fish.

**Strain** To remove the solid bits from a liquid. You know — like when you have those floaty little things you hate in your orange juice.

**Toss** Mixing enthusiastically! Yahoo!

**Whip** Like beat (see above) but even *more* so. You do this to cream and egg whites.

**Whisk** To beat with a (*surprise*) whisk. What you do to a sauce, for instance, to get the lumps out.

**Zest** The colored outside peel of an orange or lemon. Also the act of removing that part.

# The Clueless Guide to Metric Conversion

Unless you happen to be a nuclear physicist, it's not necessary to convert measurements with extreme precision. In cooking, close is usually good enough. The following tables will give you the metric equivalent for both U.S. and imperial measurements.

| METRIC CONVERSION VOLUME | | |
|---|---|---|
| **U.S. Unit** | **Imperial Unit** | **Metric Equivalent** |
| 1 U.S. gallon<br>128 fluid ounces<br>4 U.S. quarts | 1 imperial gallon<br>160 fluid ounces<br>4 imperial quarts | 4 liters |
| 1 U.S. quart<br>32 fluid ounces<br>4 cups | 1 imperial quart<br>40 fluid ounces<br>5 cups | 1 liter |
| 1 U.S. pint<br>16 fluid ounces<br>2 cups | 1 imperial pint<br>20 fluid ounces<br>2½ cups | ½ liter<br>500 milliliters |
| 1 cup<br>8 fluid ounces<br>16 tablespoons | 1 cup<br>8 fluid ounces<br>16 tablespoons | 250 milliliters |
| ½ cup<br>4 fluid ounces<br>8 tablespoons | ½ cup<br>4 fluid ounces<br>8 tablespoons | 125 milliliters |
| ¼ cup<br>2 fluid ounces<br>4 tablespoons | ¼ cup<br>2 fluid ounces<br>4 tablespoons | 60 milliliters |
| 1 tablespoon<br>3 teaspoons | 1 tablespoon<br>3 teaspoons | 15 milliliters |
| 1 teaspoon | 1 teaspoon | 5 milliliters |
| ½ teaspoon | ½ teaspoon | 2 milliliters |
| ¼ teaspoon | ¼ teaspoon | 1 milliliter |

## METRIC CONVERSION WEIGHT

| U.S. / Imperial Unit | Metric Equivalent |
|---|---|
| 2 pounds<br>32 ounces | 1 kilogram |
| 1 pound<br>16 ounces | 500 grams |
| ½ pound<br>8 ounces | 250 grams |
| ¼ pound<br>4 ounces | 125 grams |

## METRIC CONVERSION TEMPERATURE

| Fahrenheit | Celsius |
|---|---|
| 200° Fahrenheit | 100° Celsius |
| 250° Fahrenheit | 120° Celsius |
| 275° Fahrenheit | 140° Celsius |
| 300° Fahrenheit | 150° Celsius |
| 325° Fahrenheit | 160° Celsius |
| 350° Fahrenheit | 180° Celsius |
| 375° Fahrenheit | 190° Celsius |
| 400° Fahrenheit | 200° Celsius |
| 425° Fahrenheit | 220° Celsius |
| 450° Fahrenheit | 230° Celsius |

## METRIC CONVERSION PAN SIZES

| U.S. Measurement | Metric Equivalent |
|---|---|
| 8-inch pan | 20-centimeter pan |
| 9-inch pan | 23-centimeter pan |
| 10-inch pan | 25-centimeter pan |
| 9- x 13-inch pan | 23- x 33-centimeter pan |
| 10- x 15-inch pan | 35- x 40-centimeter pan |

# Index